FISH COOK

FISH COOK

from shrimp to swordfish

Aldo Zilli

Photography by David Munns

jacqui
small

First published in 2006 by Jacqui Small LLP
an imprint of Aurum Press Ltd
7 Greenland Street, London NW1 OND

This paperback edition published 2008

Publisher: Jacqui Small
Managing Editor: Kate John
Design: Janet James
Editor: Anne McDowall
Home Economist: Luisa Alves
Stylist: Roisin Nield
Production: Peter Colley

ISBN 978 1 906417 06 2

2011 2010 2009 2008

10 9 8 7 6 5 4 3 2 1

A catalogue record for this book is available from the British Library

Printed in Singapore

Half title:
Marinated anchovies, page 94

Frontispiece:
Oyster tempura, page 156

*Above, left to right: Salt cod fish
cakes with parsley sauce, page 42;
Salmon stuffed with crab and
spinach with dill sauce, page 77;
Oysters on ice with shallots, red
wine vinegar and lemon, page 157*

Right: Prawn soufflé, page 124

CONTENTS

Introduction   6

Round Fish   12

Flat Fish   50

Oily Fish   70

Exotic Fish   102

Shellfish   118

Index   158

Acknowledgements   160

INTRODUCTION

As I start writing, I couldn't be more inspired about fish. I am sitting in one of the best seafood restaurants on the Adriatic coast in the region of Abruzzo, where I was born. I am with ten English people who have bought a weekend course at my cookery school and everybody is very impressed so far. This afternoon we were at Pescara fish market, where fish is auctioned off to restaurateurs and fishmongers, and we saw the biggest octopus that I have ever seen in my life – it weighed 50kg (110lb)!

My love affair with fish started quite early in my life. When I was 11, my dad decided to move from the farm that he had managed with my mum and retire by the sea. My seven brothers, one sister and I all had to find jobs. I was the youngest and, in my school holidays, I worked for our local fishmonger – no problems with child labour in those days! At the end of my shift every week I was paid in fish, normally caught on that day – anything from sea bass to monkfish, clams or mussels. It wasn't until I was a lot older that I appreciated that early apprenticeship in cleaning and gutting fish, but my mum loved my job because it supplied her with enough food to feed all of us. Sunday lunch would normally consist of a nice, fresh, large fish with roast potatoes and salad.

We also ate a lot of blue fish, such as mackerel and sardines, which are really cheap and very good for you. Since taking part in the television show *Celebrity Fit Club*, oily fish has become a mainstay of my diet and I have noticed a big change in my life in general. I look and feel better – my skin is clearer and I now have loads more energy.

If you are buying fish to cook and eat at home, my advice is to venture into a good market, as supermarket fish counters are rarely as good or their fish as fresh. My favourite ones in London have to be Billingsgate Fish Market and Borough Market. Wherever you buy your fish, the best way of telling if it is really fresh is by its smell: a 'fishy' smell is normally an indication that it is quite old. When choosing fish, always look for bright eyes and firm flesh. If the eyes are sunk into the head, this normally means the fish has been dead for more than 48 hours. If you can see blood under the gills, the fish has not been dead for very long.

Ask for the fish to be cleaned but not necessarily filleted. Whether you are cooking sea bass, bream, mackerel, monkfish, Dover sole or even a very large fish for a dinner party, such as halibut, brill or turbot, you will find that roasting it whole not only makes a much better centrepiece, but also that most of the flavour comes from the bones.

The best cooking methods for fish are usually the most simple. One of the easiest yet most effective ways to cook a whole fish is to stuff it with rosemary and garlic and roast it with new potatoes, courgettes, onions, small Italian cherry tomatoes and a whole fresh chilli, then add a bit of water. (You can use basil or thyme instead of rosemary if you prefer.) The result will be delicious! There are, of course, many varied cooking methods for fish: one of my other favourites is barbecuing, but fish that has been poached or baked in foil or a banana leaf tastes equally good.

When cooking clams to make for your spaghetti sauce at home, don't add white wine to them: if the clams are fresh, the alcohol will take away a lot of the flavour from them, so just add water. But make sure you invest in a great bottle of extra virgin olive oil to finish off the dish. Indeed, good-quality extra virgin olive oil is an essential store-cupboard ingredient if you're going to cook fresh fish. The oil should be light green in colour and the bottle should be nice and dark. You can get a good olive oil for around £10 for 500ml (18fl oz). Whatever you do, don't cook with this olive oil though; this is just to finish off your fish dish. Buy a cheaper one for cooking. Other great ingredients for fish are lime, coriander, ginger and a little sesame oil, especially if you are marinating a fresh piece of tuna.

At my restaurant in Soho, Zilli Fish, the most popular way of eating fish, especially on a Friday, is deep-fried: we sell at least 50 servings of cod and fat chips every Friday lunchtime. Although it is traditional to eat fish on a Friday, many people don't seem to realise that you can eat cod, haddock or codling in many other ways – it doesn't have to be fried. Personally, I would prefer to eat cod that has been roasted with a little garlic, cherry tomatoes and olive oil, and, as cod is so expensive nowadays, I feel that cooking it in a deep-fat fryer is a waste. But I won't be taking the British national dish off the menu at Zilli Fish, particularly as it's a best seller! If you do order deep-fried fish and chips in a restaurant, check that the batter is a light golden colour. Unfortunately, some chefs don't change the oil in the fat fryer often

enough and it becomes dark in colour. The food shouldn't smell of oil and the chips shouldn't smell of fish, as they should be fried in different oil from the fish.

Squid is another victim of the deep-fat fryer; I tried serving it stuffed and grilled but people still prefer it deep-fried. When buying squid, make sure that the body is a nice white colour and that it doesn't smell of fish at all. Ask your fishmonger to clean the squid in front of you so that you can check the colour of the body. Squid is one of those fish that is quite difficult to cook. Cook it too little and it is rubbery; cook it too long and it becomes tough. When cooking squid to make a salad, boil it in water with a wine cork as this will make the squid tender. My favourite recipe in the book is the Grilled squid with sweet chilli sauce (see page 45). Lovely and fresh, especially when served with a rocket and Parmesan salad, it makes a great light lunch!

At my restaurant, people come to eat and be entertained and it is our job to make life easier for our customers by serving fish off the bone or as steaks – tuna, swordfish or shark. When it comes to eating shellfish – crab, lobster, langoustine, prawns, clams and mussels – the fun is in the presentation and in getting stuck in. When you order lobster, first ask the waiter to show it to you alive – it should be a light blue/black colour as lobster only turns pink when boiled – and never request it out of the shell. Simply ask for a finger bowl and make as much mess as possible – great fun!

In preparing this book, I was able to experiment with various exotic fish, such as parrot fish and pomfret, and also tried out, for me, some very different recipes, including curries and some Japanese and Chinese dishes. I had great fun and learnt a lot more about all sorts of different fish. I hope this book will inspire you, too, to cook and eat more fish and seafood. Good luck! God bless! Buon Appetito!

Carp

Catfish

Grey mullet

Gurnard

Cod

Gilt-head bream

Sea bass

Perch

Round Fish

Red mullet

Red snapper

Sea bream

Round Fish

This is an extremely large category – including such fish as cod, haddock, hake, ling, whiting, coley and mullet, to name just a few – so it would be impossible to include all of them in this book. If you come across another type of round fish that you wish to use instead of the ones I have selected for the recipes in this chapter, try and make sure that the flesh of the fish matches that of the fish I have chosen.

Round fish have an eye on either side of their head; many of their bones are attached to their fins and all will contain small pin bones. Of all the round fish, sea bass is probably the most well known. It has wonderful skin that becomes lovely and crispy when grilled or pan fried; do eat the skin as it adds to the flavour of this fish. Most round fish have white, delicate flesh, which makes them fantastic fish to roast whole with a little rosemary, garlic and lemon. Round fish are the most well known of all fish and so you are likely to have at least a general understanding of most of the fish that are featured in this chapter.

BLACK COD *Anoplopoma fimbria*
This marine fish, also known as the small scaled cod, can grow to 35cm (14in) and weigh as much as 3kg (6lb 10oz). It is not related to true cod, but is extremely good to eat.

BREAM
Most of the varieties of bream have a juicy, dense, white flesh. Most commonly available is the red sea bream (genera *Pagellus* and *Spondyliosoma*), but the gilt-head bream (*Sparus aurata*) is considered the best of all and has juicy white flesh. It is now being farmed.

CARP *Cyprinus carpio*
These hardy fish live in lakes, ponds and slow rivers, which makes them a good fish to farm. They have meaty flesh and grow to about 50cm (20in) and weigh around 3kg (6lb 10oz). The scales can be quite large; pour boiling water over to dislodge them.

CATFISH *Anarhichas lupus*
Not common in the UK, catfish are the fifth most consumed fish in the USA. Farmed catfish have a milder flavour than wild ones due to the cleaner water in which they are kept. Their very tough skin must be removed before cooking.

COD *Gadus morhua*
Cod used to be considered a cheap option, but it has been over fished and is now relatively scarce and a lot more expensive. It is a succulent fish with white flaky flesh and lends itself to most cooking methods.

COLEY *Pollachius virens*
Also called the saithe, coalfish or pollock, coley is a less well-known member of the cod family that has the same advantages as cod – firm, white, fleshy meat and almost no fat content. Lots of fish and chip shops sell this as fish and chips and it is an extremely good alternative to both cod, which is becoming increasingly expensive, and haddock.

GURNARD genus *Friglidae*
Gurnard have a relatively large bony plated head and narrow body with lots of spines. These are very sharp so be careful when cleaning. They tend to be quite cheap and are normally sold whole.

HADDOCK *Melanogrammus aeglefinus*
Part of the cod family, haddock are generally smaller than cod but can be used in the same way. Haddock is especially popular when smoked.

JOHN DORY *Zeus faber*
This fish is easily recognizable by the thumb prints on the sides of its body. It has a huge head, which, along with fins and bones, accounts for about 60 per cent of its weight.

MONKFISH *Lophius piscatorius*
This very ugly fish is almost always sold without its enormous head. It is the tail that is eaten and this has a firm, white flesh and no little bones.

MULLET
The grey mullet (*Liza auratus*) resembles sea bass but has larger scales and a smaller mouth. It lives near the sea bed, so may smell muddy. If so, soak it in water and vinegar, changing this often. Red mullet (*Mullus surmuletus*) are smaller and have a rich taste and firm flesh.

PERCH
There are two varieties: fresh water perch (*Perca fluviatilis*) and Ocean perch (*Sebastes marinus*). In season they are good pan fried; out of season use them in stews or soups.

RED SNAPPER *Lutjanus campechanis*
Found all over the world, this fish is in high demand, which has led to a high price. Red snapper has a firm texture and an almost nutty flavour. When buying look for clear, red eyes and bright red skin that fades towards the belly. Buy fillets with the skin on to help retain the flavour of the fish. Snappers are available all year round and are fantastic for grilling whole.

SEA BASS genus *Centropristis*
One the finest fish available with firm flesh, a delicate flavour and only a few small bones. Most sea bass is now farmed, but wild, line-caught fish have the best flavour. The skin of sea bass is excellent to eat but make sure you remove all the tough scales.

SHAD genus *Alosa*
Well known to fish sportsmen, shad have many bones but a delicate flavour. Long or slow cooking can soften the small bones enough to make them edible.

SQUID genus *Loligo*
These marine molluscs are found worldwide and there are numerous species. Squid are sold fresh, whole or cleaned and sliced, or frozen. They should not smell of fish: 'fishy' squid is old and will be tough. To soften, leave in a bowl of milk.

Grilled red mullet with bay leaves

When buying red mullet make sure the skin is a nice red colour and is not marked or broken. When you press down on the skin, the flesh should feel firm and not soft. This is a good fish for the barbecue or for roasting whole.

SERVES: 4

Preparation time: 5 minutes
Cooking time: 25 minutes

4 whole red mullet (400g/14oz
   each), scaled and cleaned
4 garlic cloves, crushed
4 sprigs rosemary
4 sprigs thyme
4 tablespoons olive oil
sea salt
2 garlic cloves, finely chopped
1 red chilli, seeded and finely
   chopped
1 tablespoon lemon juice
4 tablespoons finely chopped
   parsley
36 bay leaves
steamed spinach or bok choi
   to serve

method

1 Stuff each mullet with a quarter of the crushed garlic, a sprig of rosemary and a sprig of thyme, brush with olive oil and sprinkle over some sea salt.

2 Heat the remaining olive oil and cook the chopped garlic and chilli for about 5 minutes. Remove from the heat and strain. Allow to cool, then whisk in the lemon juice and parsley.

3 Brush a barbecue or grill rack with olive oil, then place the bay leaves on top to form a bed for the fish. Cook the mullet on top of the bay leaves for 10 minutes, then carefully turn them over and cook for a further 10 minutes.

4 Serve the fish on top of some steamed spinach or bok choi. Warm through the dressing and pour it over the fish.

Alternative fish:
bream, grayling, snapper

CLEANING AND GUTTING ROUND FISH

1 Using a pair of scissors, cut into the belly of the fish near the tail. Cut towards the head to make a long slash.

2 Reach into the belly, grab hold of the intestines and pull them out. Wash the inside of the fish thoroughly under cold water.

3 Using a pair of scissors, cut off all the fins.

4 Holding the tail firmly, descale the fish. Push the knife away from you and towards the head. Be careful not to cut into the flesh.

Oriental roast sea bass

I love Oriental cooking at the moment. Lots of dishes on my menu use Oriental herbs and spices and they accompany sea bass particularly well. I was inspired to make this recipe after one of my trips to my local Thai restaurant last year; now I cook it at home.

SERVES: 4

Preparation time: 10 minutes plus
    1 hour marinating time
Cooking time: 20 minutes

900g (2lb) whole sea bass, scaled
    and gutted, head on
1 garlic clove, thinly sliced
2 teaspoons soy sauce
2 tablespoons good dry white wine
1 tablespoon extra virgin olive oil
1 red chilli, seeded and finely
    chopped
1cm (½in) piece fresh root ginger,
    finely chopped
1 tablespoon roughly chopped
    coriander
rocket and Parmesan salad to serve
    (optional)

method

1 Cut 3 diagonal slices in the body of the fish and place it on a marinating tray. Push the sliced garlic into each slit. Mix together the soy sauce, white wine and olive oil and stir in the chopped chilli, ginger and coriander. Pour evenly all over the fish and leave to marinate for 1 hour. Preheat the oven to 220°C (425°F/gas 7).

2 Place a large piece of aluminium foil in a roasting tin large enough to hold the fish. Lay the fish in the centre and lift up the sides of the foil. Pour the marinade all over the fish then pinch together the edges of the foil to make a parcel.

3 Cook in the oven for 20 minutes. Remove from the oven and place the whole parcel in a large serving platter. Open the foil and serve at the table, with a rocket and Parmesan salad if desired.

Alternative fish:
grey mullet, red snapper, bream

Right: Oriental roast sea bass

Sesame baked red snapper

This is another favourite method of cooking fish; wrapping the fish helps it to retain flavour and the presentation is fantastic. I found this dish in a restaurant in Barbados where Nikki and I got married, so it has lots of memories for me.

SERVES: 4

Preparation time: 10 minutes plus
    4–5 hours marinating time
Cooking time: 35 minutes

2 tablespoons vegetable oil
2 teaspoons sesame oil
2 teaspoons sesame seeds
2.5cm (1in) piece fresh root ginger,
    very thinly sliced
2 garlic cloves, crushed
2 small red chillies, seeded and
    finely chopped
1 medium onion, sliced
2 tablespoons white wine
1 tablespoon nam pla (fish sauce)
2 teaspoons caster sugar
½ teaspoon cracked pepper
juice of 2 limes
2–4 banana leaves (optional)
2 whole red snapper (400g/
    14oz each)

Stir-fried vegetables
1 tablespoon olive oil
1 garlic clove, crushed
2 red peppers, cut into strips
2 yellow peppers, cut into strips
1 red onion, cut into strips
2 courgettes, cut into strips

Mango crisps
vegetable oil for deep frying
1 mango, skin left on, sliced thinly
flour for dusting

method

1 To make the marinade, heat the vegetable oil and sesame oil in a wok or pan, add the sesame seeds and fry until golden. Add the ginger, garlic, chilli and onion and cook over a low heat. Stir in the wine, nam pla, sugar, pepper and lime juice. Simmer for about 2–3 minutes and then remove from heat, set aside to cool.

2 If you are using banana leaves, make sure to soften the central stem by dipping it in boiling water then rubbing it with vegetable oil to keep the leaf flexible. Banana leaves are inedible, but they will flavour the fish. Alternatively you can use aluminium foil.

3 Spread the marinade over the fish and then wrap them in banana leaves. Thread the leaves with bamboo skewers to keep the leaf together. Place in the fridge or another cool place and leave to marinate for 4–5 hours. If using foil roll the edges to form a parcel.

4 Preheat the oven to 180°C (350°F/gas 4). Place the fish parcels on a baking tray and cook for 35 minutes. (Allow a longer cooking time if your fish are larger than 400g/14oz.)

5 Meanwhile, make the mango crisps. Heat the vegetable oil in a frying pan, dust the mango slices with flour and deep fry until light golden. Drain on some paper towels and keep warm.

6 A few minutes before the fish is cooked, stir-fry the vegetables. Heat the olive oil, add the garlic to the pan and cook for 1 minute. Remove the garlic from the pan, then add the red and yellow pepper, red onion and courgettes and stir fry for 3 minutes.

7 Remove the fish from the oven and carefully open the parcels. Serve in the middle of the table with the stir-fried vegetables and mango crisps.

Alternative fish:
mullet, grayling, snapper, parrot
fish, monkfish tails

Bream stuffed with thyme and pan fried in lemon oil

I grew up near the Adriatic Sea and at home we always cooked with whole fish as my mother used to say that the bones gave the fish more flavour. To this day it is still one of my favourite ways of cooking fish.

SERVES: 4

Preparation time: 10 minutes
Cooking time: 25 minutes

3 tablespoons chopped dill
2 tablespoons chopped rosemary
4 tablespoons chopped parsley
2 teaspoons chopped thyme
½ teaspoon salt
½ teaspoon ground black pepper
2 small whole bream (500g/
    1lb 2oz each)
2 lemons, sliced
115ml (4fl oz) extra virgin olive oil
6 tablespoons lemon juice
4 tablespoons white wine

method

1 Preheat the oven to 180°C (350°F/gas 4). Mix the chopped dill, rosemary, parsley, thyme, salt and pepper and fill each cavity with a slice of lemon and this herb mixture.

2 Heat the oil in a frying pan and pan fry the fish for 5 minutes on each side. Add the lemon juice to the pan and cook for a further 3 minutes on each side.

3 Place the fish on a roasting tray in the oven and bake for 9 minutes.

4 Remove the fish to a plate and then add the white wine to the pan to deglaze. Pour the sauce over the fish and serve immediately with some extra lemon slices.

Alternative fish:
sea bass, grayling

Shad stuffed with sorrel and served with beurre blanc

Sorrel is half vegetable and half herb with a strong, very lemony flavour that marries well with fish. Basil and cherry tomatoes in season make a great salad to serve with any fish and one that complements this dish beautifully.

SERVES: 4

Preparation time: 10 minutes
Cooking time: 20 minutes

4 whole shad (250g/9oz each) or
    4 shad fillets (175g/6oz each)
2 tablespoons chopped fresh sorrel
2 garlic cloves, finely chopped
2 tablespoons olive oil

Sauce
3 shallots, finely diced
5 tablespoons white wine
5 tablespoons white wine vinegar
115g (4oz) unsalted butter, diced
    and chilled
1 teaspoon lemon juice
salt and freshly ground black pepper

method

1 Preheat the oven to 190°C (375°F/gas 5). If you are using whole fish, stuff the cavity of each with a mixture of sorrel and garlic. If using fillets, place a mixture of garlic and sorrel in the middle of each fillet and roll, securing each with a cocktail stick.

2 Place the whole fish or rolled fillets onto a greased baking tray and pour the olive oil all over the fish. Bake in the oven for 20 minutes (for whole fish, or 15 minutes if using fish fillets).

3 Meanwhile, make the sauce: simmer the shallots, wine and vinegar in a saucepan until reduced to about 3 tablespoons of liquid. Remove and set aside to cool for at least 15 minutes.

4 Whisk in the butter, adding it slowly, making sure the butter is completely incorporated before adding any more, to make a pale sauce. Add the lemon juice and season to taste. Leave until ready to be gently reheated to add to the fish.

5 Remove the fish from the oven and pour the hot sauce over.

Alternative fish:
mullet, salmon

Right: Shad stuffed with sorrel and served with beurre blanc

STUFFING A WHOLE FISH

1 Lay the cleaned fish on a board and lift up one side to create an opening. Stuff with lemon and herbs, making sure to fill all the cavity.

FILLETING ROUND FISH

1 Using scissors, snip the fins off the fish. Lift one side of the fish and with a sharp knife trim the fat from the belly, working from head to tail.

2 Turn the fish over and remove the fat from the other side in the same way. Discard the fat.

3 Open out the fish with the skin side up. Using the knife, cut the flesh away from the back bone, working down towards the tail.

4 Turn the fish over and cut the fillet away from the fish. Repeat steps 3 and 4 on the other side to remove the second fillet.

Baked cod with black olive crust and lentils

I first came up with this recipe when I took part in the TV show *Celebrity Fit Club*; it helped me to lose weight as it is low in calories and has good nutritional value with iron and lots of protein.

SERVES: 4

Preparation time: 15 minutes
Cooking time: 40 minutes

100ml (3½fl oz) extra virgin olive oil
1 carrot, diced
1 stick celery, diced
1 onion, chopped
500g (1lb 2oz) lentils, soaked
   overnight if dried
2 bay leaves
1.5 litres (2¾ pints) vegetable stock
1 tablespoon breadcrumbs
1 teaspoon each rosemary and thyme
100g (3½oz) stoned black olives
4 cod fillets (175g/6oz each)

method

1 Heat half the oil in a large pan and add the carrot, celery and onion. Cook until soft, about 3–4 minutes, stirring to ensure they don't stick.

2 Add the lentils and bay leaves, stir a couple of times and then add the stock and cook until it has been absorbed by the lentils, about 30 minutes. Preheat oven to 180°C (350°F/gas 4).

3 Meanwhile, in a food processor, blend the remaining oil, the breadcrumbs, rosemary, thyme and black olives until you have a smooth mix.

4 Place the cod fillets in a roasting tray and divide the olive mixture between them. Press down with your fingers and ensure it covers the fillets. Bake in the oven for 7–8 minutes. Serve fish on a bed of lentils.

Alternative fish:

mackerel, salmon, John Dory, halibut

Pan-fried perch with béarnaise sauce

Normally you associate this sauce with a good steak so a good alternative to perch would be tuna. If you use tuna for this recipe, make sure the pan is smoking hot before you add the tuna and then only sear it.

SERVES: 4

Preparation time: 10 minutes
Cooking time: 20 minutes

4 perch fillets (185g/6½oz each)
1 tablespoon olive oil

Sauce
55g (2oz) shallots, minced
125ml (4½fl oz) tarragon wine
   vinegar
3 tablespoons finely chopped fresh
   tarragon
pinch of cracked black peppercorns
6 egg yolks
700g (1lb 8oz) clarified butter, hot
salt to taste
cayenne pepper to taste
fresh lemon juice to taste

method

1 To make the béarnaise sauce, mix together shallots, vinegar, 2 tablespoons tarragon and peppercorns in a stainless steel pan and simmer until reduced by two thirds. Remove from heat and set aside to cool for 15 minutes.

2 Transfer to a heat-resistant bowl, add the egg yolks and whisk well. Place the bowl over a pan of simmering water and continue to whisk the sauce until thick and creamy. Be careful that the eggs do not scramble; remove the bowl from heat if you think this is happening.

3 Remove the sauce from the heat and, continuing to whisk, gradually add the hot clarified butter. If the sauce becomes too thick then thin with a little lemon juice or water. Strain the sauce through a muslin cloth and season to taste with salt, cayenne pepper and lemon juice. Add the remaining tarragon.

4 Pan fry the perch fillets in olive oil for 8 minutes on each side. Reheat the béarnaise sauce and serve with the fish.

Alternative fish:
tuna, monkfish

Left: Baked cod with black olive crust and lentils

1 Lay the fish on a board and snip off the spiny fins with a pair of scissors.

2 Lifting the gill fin, make a diagonal cut to the top of the head behind the fin.

3 Insert the knife halfway down the backbone, keeping as close to the bone as possible, and cut towards the tail.

4 Keeping the knife flat, continue to cut round the fish until you have separated the entire fillet.

John Dory with tapenade, mash and spinach

John Dory are easily distinguished from other similar fish by a black spot known as 'St Peter's Thumb'. The story goes that St Peter picked up this fish and left this black mark on its body. It is a great tasting fish and works really well with these ingredients. To serve, arrange the mash, spinach and fish fillet on each plate in a little tower.

SERVES: 4

Cooking time: 15 minutes
Preparation time: 20 minutes

4 John Dory fillets (225g/8oz each)
6 tablespoons olive oil
40g (1½oz) unsalted butter
1 tablespoon lemon juice
1 glass dry white wine
450g (1lb) potatoes, peeled and
   quartered
1.2kg (2lb 10oz) spinach, washed
   and tough stalks removed
2 garlic cloves, peeled and crushed
1 fresh red chilli, seeded and finely
   chopped
salt and freshly ground black pepper
milk (as necessary for mash)
extra virgin olive oil to serve

Alternative fish:
skate, snapper

Tapenade
100g (3½oz) stoned black olives
1 garlic clove, peeled and chopped
25g (1oz) fresh anchovy fillets,
   drained
15g (½oz) capers
squeeze lemon juice
3 fresh basil leaves
1 tablespoon olive oil
freshly ground black pepper

method

1 Make the tapenade first. Place all the ingredients in a food processor and blitz until all are roughly chopped and combined. Set aside for the flavours to infuse.

2 Pan fry the fillets skin side down in 3 tablespoons of olive oil and 25g (1oz) of the butter for 3 minutes. Add the lemon juice and wine and cook for a further 2 minutes. Turn over the fillets and fry on the other side for a further 5 minutes. If the pan is getting too dry, add a little more olive oil and lemon juice.

3 Boil the potatoes for 10 minutes until soft enough to mash.

4 Meanwhile, place the spinach leaves in a large heavy-based saucepan (do not add water). Cover the pan and cook gently for 6–7 minutes until the spinach wilts, stirring occasionally to prevent it from sticking to the pan. Drain well and allow to cool slightly, then squeeze out excess water. Chop roughly.

5 Heat 3 tablespoons of oil in the same pan. Stir in the garlic and chilli and fry for 2 minutes. Add the spinach, season to taste and cook until the spinach is heated through.

6 Mash potatoes with remaining butter and milk and season to taste. To serve, place the mash on each plate, top with the spinach, then place a fillet in the centre of each. Spoon over the tapenade and drizzle with extra virgin olive oil.

5 Lift up the fillet and carefully slide the knife along the bone to release it completely.

6 Be careful of any pin bones that may remain in the fillet. You will need to remove these with tweezers.

7 The fillet will come away in one piece. Turn the fish over and repeat steps 2–6 on the other side.

8 Tidy up each fillet and cut into pieces as required. The fillets will not be equal in size and shape, but this is normal.

1 Lay 3 strips of Parma ham or bacon side by side on a board. Place the fillet and any other fillings across the Parma ham strips at one end.

2 Lift up the ends of the Parma ham, lay them over the top of the fillings and pat down. Pull towards you and roll tightly at the same time.

3 Continue rolling tightly until you reach the end. Lay the wrapped fillet on a board with ends underneath until ready to cook.

Monkfish wrapped in Parma ham

Bacon is a good alternative to Parma ham. If you can't find monkfish fillets make sure that the fish you choose instead has suitably firm flesh.

SERVES: 4–6

Preparation time: 20 minutes
Cooking time: 20 minutes

½ small red pepper
½ small green pepper
½ small yellow pepper
2 monkfish fillets (350g/12oz) each
125g (4½oz) Parma ham, sliced
1 large sprig rosemary, separated into small sprigs
4 tablespoons extra virgin olive oil
sliced red onions and tomatoes

Sauce
175ml (6fl oz) Champagne
3 tablespoons fruit vinegar
125ml (4½fl oz) fish stock
3 teaspoons caster sugar
4 tablespoons fresh mint leaves, finely chopped
2 tablespoons unsalted butter

Alternative fish:
Dover sole, turbot

method

1 Preheat the oven to 200°C (400°F/gas 6). Cut away the membranes from the peppers, then slice the peppers very finely into strips. Season the monkfish all over.

2 Lay the Parma ham out flat on a work surface with each slice slightly overlapping, then arrange half of the peppers along the centre. Place the monkfish fillets on top and lay the remaining pepper slices and half of the rosemary sprigs on the fish. Tightly roll the Parma ham around the monkfish, then pierce the rolls with the remaining rosemary sprigs to secure them.

3 Heat a large heavy-based ovenproof frying pan until hot, add the olive oil and heat until hot. Add the monkfish and seal for 5 minutes, turning the fish constantly.

4 Transfer the pan to the oven and roast for 10 minutes, then turn off the oven and open the door slightly; this will keep the fish warm while you are making the sauce.

5 To make the sauce, place the Champagne in a pan over medium heat and simmer for 6 minutes, then add the vinegar, stock, sugar and half the mint. Simmer until the liquid is reduced by half. Over a low heat, whisk in the butter, then stir in the remaining mint.

6 Serve the fish on top of sliced red onions and tomatoes with the sauce on the side.

Tahini baked haddock

Again this is quite a healthy recipe; I cook it at home quite often and Nikki loves it. This dish is great served with some organic houmous and rocket. Don't be afraid to try this recipe – it is incredibly simple and tasty.

SERVES. 4

Preparation time: 10 minutes
Cooking time: 35 minutes

4 haddock fillets (350–400g/
    12–14oz each)
juice of 2 lemons
2 tablespoons extra virgin olive oil
1 cup tahini
1 garlic clove, finely chopped
4 tablespoons water
2 white onions, sliced
couscous or rice and a herb salad
    to serve (optional)

method

1 Preheat the oven to 200°C (400°F/gas 6). Place a sheet of aluminium foil on the base of a baking tray or dish and place the haddock fillets on top of the foil. Mix together 1 tablespoon of lemon juice and 1 tablespoon of olive oil and pour the mixture over the fish. Place another piece of foil over the fish and seal the edges to form a parcel. Bake for 15 minutes.

2 Meanwhile mix together the tahini and garlic. In another bowl, combine the remaining lemon juice and the water. Slowly add the lemon juice mix to the tahini, then beat with a whisk until smooth and creamy. Season with salt and freshly ground black pepper to taste.

3 Pan fry the onions in the remaining olive oil until brown and almost crispy.

4 Remove the fish from the oven and pull off the top layer of foil. Place the onions around the fish and then pour over the tahini mixture and bake for a further 15 minutes, or until the topping is bubbling and a lovely golden colour. (Do not replace the foil as you want the fish to start browning). Serve with some couscous or rice and a herb salad if desired.

Alternative fish:
cod, coley, John Dory, codling

Sea bream with mozzarella and pancetta

This summer when I was back in Italy I went to dinner at one of my friends' and his wife was preparing this amazing recipe because the Campania region is where they make the best mozzarella in the world. You won't know how good this recipe is until you try it so please go for it, make sure you use a good buffalo mozzarella.

SERVES: 4

Preparation time: 30 minutes
Cooking time: 20 minutes

4 x 225g whole sea bream, filleted
  and skinned
3 tablespoons extra virgin olive oil
1 tablespoon lemon juice
200g buffalo mozzarella
8 basil leaves
squeeze of lemon juice
freshly ground black pepper
8 slices of pancetta
100g new potatoes cut into slices
sea salt and ground black pepper

Alternative fish:
sea bass or swordfish

method

1 Lay one sea bream fillet on a board and with a round pastry cutter or knife cut a circle in the fillet. Repeat with the other fillet. Place a slice of buffalo mozzarella on top and then a couple of basil leaves, drizzle with olive oil and then place the other fillet on top of the mozzarella. Lay another slice of mozzarella on top.

2 Take two slices of pancetta and wrap around the sea bream to encase the tower.

3 Place the sea bream on a greased baking tray, drizzle with the extra virgin olive oil, lemon juice and season with salt and pepper, cook in a 180°C oven for 20 minutes. Serve on top of some dressed rocket with a drizzle of vintage balsamic vinegar.

Cod in teriyaki and mango

Teriyaki is my new favourite flavour for food, especially with fish. If you choose to use black cod it is quite difficult to find fresh, so buy it frozen. It is one of the few fish that I don't mind buying frozen as the flavour remains just as good as that of a fresh fish.

SERVES: 4

Preparation time: 15 minutes plus 20 minutes marinating time
Cooking time: 25 minutes

3 tablespoons teriyaki sauce
2 tablespoons red curry paste
2 tablespoons caster sugar
8 kaffir lime leaves
4 teaspoons chopped coriander
4 teaspoons chopped spring onions
2 mangoes, chopped
4 thick pieces of cod (275g/ 10oz each)
4 large banana leaves
4 blanched savoy cabbage leaves

Salsa
1 red onion, finely chopped
2 tablespoons finely chopped coriander
1 mango, finely chopped
2 tablespoons extra virgin olive oil
1 avocado, finely chopped
juice of 1 lemon
juice of 1 lime
salt and freshly ground black pepper

method

1 First make the marinade: combine the teriyaki sauce, red curry paste, sugar, lime leaves, half the coriander and half the spring onions and the chopped mango. Add the cod to the marinade and leave for 15–20 minutes. Preheat the oven to 190°C (375°F/gas 5).

2 To make the salsa, mix together all the ingredients in a bowl and leave in the fridge until ready to use.

3 Remove the fish steaks from the marinade, place each onto the centre of a banana leaf and cover with remaining marinade. Wrap the edges of the leaves over the fish and secure in place with a cocktail stick.

4 Bake the fish in the oven for 15 minutes, then open the parcels and return them to the oven for a further 10 minutes.

5 To serve, place each fish steak on a blanched savoy cabbage leaf, sprinkle with the remaining coriander and spring onions and serve immediately with the salsa.

Alternative fish:
black cod, sea bass

1 Place the fish fillet in a deep pan of boiling liquid; make sure there is enough liquid to cover all the fillets. Simmer for about 10 minutes.

Carp poached in beer

This is a very simple recipe but it is delicious. Another good way of cooking this fish is to deep fry it in beer batter, but this recipe is definitely healthier for you.

SERVES: 4

Preparation time: 5 minutes
Cooking time: 30 minutes

2 x 300ml (10fl oz) bottles beer
1 medium onion, sliced
1 garlic clove, crushed
2 bay leaves
2 sticks celery, diced
2 teaspoons salt
1 teaspoon cracked black pepper
4 carp fillets (175g/6oz each)
1 lemon, quartered
sliced roast potatoes to serve
    (optional)

method

1 Pour the beer into a deep frying pan and add the onion, garlic, bay leaves, celery and salt and pepper.

2 Bring to the boil and simmer for 10 minutes, then add the carp and lemon and simmer for a further 12 minutes.

3 Remove the carp and reduce the beer by three quarters. Pour over the fish and serve on top of sliced roasted potatoes if desired.

Alternative fish:
trout, catfish, eel

Sour orange coley

This is a good dish to share in the middle of the table when you have friends around. It is a fairly mild curry so feel free to add extra chillies if you want to give it a little kick!

SERVES: 4

Preparation time: 10 minutes
Cooking time: 25 minutes

300ml (10fl oz) fish stock
pinch of sea salt
6 savoy cabbage leaves
    (or Chinese leaves), torn
1 teaspoon nam pla (fish sauce)
4 coley fillets (175g/6oz each)
mint leaves
cooked coconut rice to serve

Curry paste
4 large chillies, seeded and
    chopped
4 shallots, chopped
2 garlic cloves, chopped
1 tablespoon shrimp paste
½ teaspoon salt
½ teaspoon sugar
½ teaspoon turmeric
2 tablespoons ground nut or
    sesame oil
½ teaspoon chopped fresh root
    ginger

method

1 Blend all the curry paste ingredients until smooth, transfer to a pan and bring to the boil. Cook for 3 minutes, stirring continuously.

2 Add half the fish stock and a pinch of sea salt, bring back to the boil, then add the cabbage and cook for a further 8 minutes. Add remaining stock and the fish sauce, bring back to the boil and cook for 5 minutes.

3 Add the coley fillets and simmer for 4–5 minutes. Remove the cooked fish and keep warm. Add mint leaves to the sauce and cook for 4 minutes.

4 To serve, divide the coconut rice between 4 serving plates, pour over the curry sauce and top with the fish.

Alternative fish:
cod, codling, monkfish

Left: Carp poached in beer

Steamed sea bass with Thai herbs

You can't really go wrong when cooking sea bass as it is such a great fish. Try and find wild sea bass in the summer season, as the taste is much stronger and the flesh is much firmer.

SERVES: 4

Preparation time: 5 minutes
Cooking time: 20 minutes

1 teaspoon grated fresh root ginger
1 teaspoon chopped coriander
1 teaspoon finely chopped lemongrass
1 teaspoon nam pla (fish sauce)
pinch of brown sugar
1 bunch spring onions, finely chopped
1 chilli, finely chopped
4 banana leaves
4 sea bass fillets (200g/7oz each)
soy sauce and steamed bok choi to
    serve (optional)

Alternative fish:
sea bream,
grey mullet

method

1 In a bowl stir together the ginger, coriander, lemongrass, fish sauce, sugar, spring onions and chilli until well combined.

2 Line the bottom of a steamer with banana leaves and place the fish fillets on top. Cover the top of the fillets with the herb mixture, making sure they are well coated. Steam the fish for 20 minutes.

3 Serve on top of the banana leaves with a little soy sauce and some steamed bok choi if desired.

Spiced monkfish wrapped in Chinese leaves

Monkfish is a very ugly looking fish so you never see it in supermarkets with the head still on. It is a great firm fish for roasting, very much like meat. This recipe, which would also be great served with bok choi or stir-fried vegetables, came from London's Chinatown, where I tend to eat quite often.

SERVES: 4

Preparation time: 15 minutes
Cooking time: 20 minutes

1cm (½in) piece fresh root ginger,
   peeled and finely chopped
2 whole chillies, finely chopped
2 stalks lemongrass, finely chopped
2 tablespoons chopped coriander
2 tablespoons sesame oil
1 teaspoon soy sauce
200g (7oz) Chinese leaves, blanched
2 monkfish fillets (300g/10½oz each)
mashed potatoes or salad to serve
   (optional)

method

1 Preheat the oven to 180°C (350°F/gas 4). Blend the ginger, chilli, lemongrass, coriander, sesame oil and soy sauce in a food processor.

2 Take a large sheet of cling film and place the Chinese leaves on top in an overlapping fashion. Place the monkfish in the middle of the leaves and brush with the herb mixture. Pour over any remaining herb mixture. Wrap the leaves around the fish and then wrap the cling film over the whole parcel. Place this on a large piece of aluminium foil, wrap around the monkfish and pinch at both ends to form a cracker shape.

3 Bake the parcel in the oven for 20 minutes, then remove from the oven and remove and discard foil and film. Slice the monkfish into medallions and pour the cooking juices over the fish. Serve with mashed potatoes or salad if desired.

Alternative fish:
sea bass, swordfish, tuna

Gurnard bouillabaisse

Where I grew up in Italy this fish was very popular, but in England it is less so, mainly because of all the bones.
It is, however, great for soups and stews. In season, it is fantastic just roasted with some garlic and potatoes.

SERVES: 4

Preparation time: 10 minutes
Cooking time: 40 minutes

125ml (4½fl oz) olive oil
3 onions, finely chopped
2 garlic cloves, chopped
2 leeks, chopped (white part only)
450g (1lb) fresh ripe tomatoes,
    peeled and chopped
2 litres (3½ pints) fish stock
1 sachet saffron
2 bay leaves
2 sprigs fresh thyme

1.5kg (3lb 8oz) gurnard meat,
    chopped into chunks
4 potatoes, peeled and sliced fairly
    thickly
salt and freshly ground black pepper
pinch of cayenne pepper

Alternative fish:
grey mullet, sea bream

method

1 In a large pan, heat the oil and then add the onions, garlic, leeks and tomatoes and cook until soft. Add the fish stock, saffron, bay leaves and thyme and boil for 15–20 minutes. Lower the heat and then add the fish and potatoes.

2 Simmer for 5–8 minutes, removing the fish as it is cooked and keeping it on the side; cook until the potatoes are very tender and falling apart. Season with salt, pepper and cayenne.

3 Divide the fish stew between 4 bowls. If you prefer, you could strain the the stew into bowls and serve as a soup with garlic croutons.

Fish pie

This is a great alternative to shepherd's pie but a lot lighter. Fish pie is a great comfort food and I highly recommend this recipe for those chilly winter nights.

SERVES: 4

Preparation time: 20 minutes
Cooking time: 35 minutes

250g (9oz) cod fillets
225g (8oz) smoked haddock or cod
    fillets
150ml (5fl oz) milk
150ml (5fl oz) water
1 teaspoon black peppercorns
1 lemon, cut in half
1 bay leaf
1 sprig lemon thyme
85g (3oz) unsalted butter
25g (1oz) flour
3 tablespoons freshly chopped
    parsley
salt and freshly ground black pepper
450g (1lb) potatoes, peeled and cut
    into quarters
about 3 tablespoons milk
100g (3½oz) raw salmon, diced
100g (3½oz) raw prawns, chopped
3 eggs, hard boiled and roughly
    chopped
115g (4oz) grated cheese

Alternative fish:
any fish fillets,
including smoked
(e.g. herring,
mackerel, sardine)

method

1 Place the cod, smoked fish, milk, water, peppercorns, lemon, bay leaf and thyme in a saucepan and bring to the boil. Reduce the heat and simmer for 8 minutes until the fish is nearly cooked. Strain, reserving the cooking liquid. When the fish is cool, remove skin and bones and flake the flesh into a bowl. Preheat the oven to 200°C (400°F/gas 6).

2 Melt 25g (1oz) of the butter in a small pan and add the flour. Stir continuously and cook for about 1 minute. Gradually add the reserved cooking liquid, stirring (or whisking) all the time to prevent it becoming lumpy. Stir in the parsley and season with salt and pepper.

3 Meanwhile cook the potatoes in boiling water until soft (about 10–15 minutes), then drain and mash with 25g (1oz) butter and about 3 tablespoons of milk and season to taste.

4 Add the raw salmon and prawns to the cooked fish and then add the eggs and white sauce. Mix together using a wooden spoon and transfer to an ovenproof dish.

5 Spread the mashed potato over the fish mixture, dot with the remaining butter and sprinkle with grated cheese. Cook for about 20–25 minutes until the top is golden and the inside bubbling

FRYING FISH FILLETS

1 Dip the fish fillet in flour, breadcrumbs or ground nuts. Make sure it is completely coated on both sides.

2 Heat some oil or butter in a deep, non-stick frying pan until very hot. Carefully lay the fillet in the oil and fry for about 7 minutes.

3 Using a slotted spoon turn the fish fillet carefully and cook the other side for about 7 minutes.

4 Once golden brown, lift off the pan using a slotted spoon or fish slice and allow oil to drain off.

Catfish in cornmeal

This is not a fish I would normally choose to serve in my restaurants, but after we shot the photo opposite, I put this dish on the menu and it worked a treat with the customers. Catfish is very well known in the USA; let's hope it catches on in the rest of the world too. Ask your fishmonger to prepare the fish for you as there is a lot to do to it.

SERVES: 4

Preparation time: 10 minutes
Cooking time: 15 minutes

4 tablespoons cornmeal
2 tablespoons finely ground pine nuts
2 tablespoons flour
pinch of salt
½ teaspoon cayenne pepper
½ teaspoon cumin
4 catfish fillets (175g/6oz each)
4 tablespoons olive oil
minted new potatoes and balsamic vinegar to serve (optional)

method

1 In a flat dish combine the cornmeal, pine nuts, flour, salt, cayenne pepper and cumin.

2 Dip the catfish fillets in the cornmeal mixture, making sure they are well coated, and place them on another plate.

3 Heat the oil in a heavy-based pan until very hot. Lay the catfish fillets in the oil and fry for about 7 minutes on each side or until golden brown. Serve with minted new potatoes and balsamic vinegar, if desired.

Alternative fish:
tuna, shark, swordfish, barracuda

Deep-fried cod and chips

Cod is one of my favourite fish and when available I like to treat myself to this great recipe, which also works really well with coley or haddock.

SERVES: 4

Preparation time: 20 minutes
Cooking time: 28 minutes

4 x 200g fillets of cod, skin on
1 tablespoon sea salt flakes
2 lemons cut in half

Tartar sauce
makes 150ml (5fl oz)
150ml (5fl oz) mayonnaise
1 shallot, finely chopped
15ml (1 tablespoon) finely chopped
    fresh flat-leaf parsley
15ml (1 tablespoon) capers, rinsed,
    patted dry with kitchen paper
    and chopped
2 small gherkins, finely diced

Batter
120ml beer
120ml sparkling water
1 tablespoon olive oil
1 teaspoon sea salt
140g self-raising flour

Chips
900g (2lb) Maris Piper, peeled
groundnut oil for deep-frying
sea salt flakes

method

1 Pour the beer and water into a bowl, add the oil and salt and whisk until combined. Add the flour and whisk slowly until mixed, batter should be smooth, but don't over work it. If the batter is too thick add a teaspoon of water at a time until you reach a pancake batter consistency.

2 Mix together all the ingredients for the tartar sauce. Serve immediately or chill, covered with cling film, in the fridge until required.

3 Cut the potatoes to your desired thickness and wash in cold water. Place in a bowl of cold water and leave to stand for 10 minutes. Drain and dry thoroughly with a clean tea towel. Pour enough oil for deep-frying into a deep-frying pan. Heat to about 165°C before adding the chips. Blanch the chips first in the oil for 4–5 minutes, then remove (the chips should just yield to the touch). Heat the oil to about 195°C, add the chips and cook for 5–8 minutes to crisp and turn golden brown. Using a slotted spoon, transfer the chips to kitchen paper to drain and season with sea salt.

4 Dip the cod into flour and then holding the edges dip into the batter turning once. Cook in hot oil (155°C) for 20 minutes, turning occasionally.

5 Remove from the oil into a bowl lined with paper towels, sprinkle with sea salt and serve immediately with the chips, tartar sauce and lemon.

Alternative fish:
coley or haddock

1 Lay the rehydrated cod on the board skin side down and with a knife lift up the fat and cut it away from the flesh of the fish.

2 Remove all the fat down the side so that you end up with a trimmed fillet. Discard the fat.

3 Insert a sharp knife between the skin and the fish and cut along the skin, lifting the fillet off as you go along.

4 Cut the fish into bite-sized pieces ready to make your stew, or cut it into large fillet portions to pan fry, roast or grill.

Salt cod caldeirada

I picked this recipe up on holiday in Portugal and was inspired to make my own version of it. I hope you enjoy making it for friends – it's superb for Sunday lunch.

SERVES: 4

Preparation time: 10 minutes
Cooking time: 1 hour

1 tablespoon extra virgin olive oil
2 garlic cloves, finely chopped
1 large white onion, sliced
6 potatoes
8 tomatoes
1 spicy chorizo sausage
700g (1lb 8oz) salt cod, rehydrated
8 raw tiger prawns
½ teaspoon paprika
2 bay leaves
1 teaspoon oregano
chopped parsley to serve

method

1 In a large deep saucepan, heat the olive oil and pan fry the garlic and onion for 1 minute over a medium heat. Remove from the heat.

2 Peel and slice the potatoes into 2cm (¾in) widths, peel and roughly chop the tomatoes, slice the chorizo sausage and peel and devein the tiger prawns. Cut the rehydrated salt cod into large chunks.

3 Add the potatoes, tomatoes, chorizo sausage, prawns and salt cod to the pan, along with the paprika, bay leaves and oregano. Pour in enough water to just cover the ingredients.

4 Return to the heat and simmer for 1 hour until the potatoes are tender. Serve scattered with chopped parsley.

Alternative fish:
monkfish, John Dory, bream

1 Place the salt cod in a bowl of cold water and leave to soak for 24 hours to rehydrate it and remove salt. Change the water frequently.

2 Cook fish in a saucepan of fresh boiling water for 20–30 minutes. Drain and cool, remove skin and bones and flake the fish into a bowl.

3 Add the remaining ingredients to the bowl and mash until all the ingredients are combined.

4 Flour your hands and, taking a handful of fish mixture at a time, roll it into a ball. Gently flatten it to make a round 'cake'.

Salt cod fish cakes with parsley sauce

This is one of my favourite photos in the book: I love the crunchy vegetables the fish cakes are served with. This is a great dish to serve a family and you can vary it by serving the fish cakes with chilli sauce instead of this parsley one.

SERVES: 4

Preparation time: 15 minutes plus 24 hours soaking time
Cooking time: 1 hour

250g (9oz) salt cod
450g (1lb) potatoes, peeled and chopped
½ teaspoon cayenne pepper
1 chilli, seeded and finely chopped
3 garlic cloves, finely chopped
2 tablespoons finely chopped parsley
55ml (2fl oz) single cream
2 egg yolks
100g (3½oz) plain flour
1 tablespoon olive oil
100g (3½oz) butter
stir-fried vegetables to serve

Parsley sauce
40g (1½oz) unsalted butter
40g (1½oz) plain flour
300ml (10fl oz) milk, warm
300ml (10fl oz) fish stock, warm
5 tablespoons finely chopped parsley
salt and freshly ground black pepper

method

1 Soak the cod in cold water for at least 24 hours, changing the water 4 or 5 times.

2 Drain the fish and place in a saucepan, cover with fresh water and simmer over medium heat for 20–30 minutes until it is cooked. Drain and, when cool, flake the fish into a large bowl, making sure to remove the skin and any bones.

3 Meanwhile cook the potatoes in salted water for 10–15 minutes until they are soft. Drain and push potatoes through a sieve or a potato ricer.

4 Add the potato to the cod along with the cayenne pepper, chilli, garlic, parsley, cream and egg yolks and mix well to combine. Flour your hands and then pick up some of the fish mixture and roll it in your hands to make a ball. On a floured board, flatten the ball down slightly to make a fish cake shape – you can make either two small fish cakes or one large one per person. These can be covered and kept in the fridge for up to 12 hours before cooking.

5 To make the parsley sauce, melt the butter in a saucepan over a low heat and then stir in the flour using a wooden spoon to make a roux. Gradually add the warm milk and fish stock a little at a time, stirring continuously to make sure the sauce is smooth with no lumps. Bring to the boil and, continuing to stir, simmer the sauce for 5 minutes until smooth and creamy. Remove from the heat, add the parsley and season to taste. (This can be reheated when you need it.)

6 Pan fry the fish cakes in the olive oil and butter over a medium heat for about 15 minutes (depending on the size of your fish cakes), turning once, until golden brown. Serve on top of some stir-fried seasonal vegetables with the sauce poured around.

Alternative fish:
cod, salmon, crab meat

Sashimi of sea bass

Sashimi is any kind of fresh, raw fillet of fish that is not served with rice – other sushi are served either with or on rice. Make sure that you ask your fishmonger for sushi-grade fish when you are making this recipe; this will guarantee the freshness of the fish. It is important to find very fresh fish for sashimi dishes.

SERVES: 4

Preparation time: 10 minutes plus
   45 minutes marinating time

150g (5½oz) very fresh sea bass
3 tablespoons soy sauce
1 teaspoon wasabi
2 ripe avocados
4 shiso leaves
1 tablespoon toasted sesame seeds

Alternative fish:
salmon, tuna

method

1 Slice the sea bass very thinly.

2 Mix together the soy and wasabi and marinate the sea bass in this mixture.

3 Stone and peel the avocado and cut into chunks.

4 Lay the sea bass on a flat plate and place the avocado on top. Sprinkle with the shiso and sesame seeds. Pour over some of the marinade before eating.

Smoked haddock and avocado mousse

Smoked fish is quite under-rated nowadays: I remember it as a delicacy and still treat it like one. When I was working in the south of France this recipe was always on the menu; I decided to include it here as it's a great, easy recipe.

SERVES: 4

Preparation time: 20 minutes
Cooking time: 15 minutes
Chilling time: 1 hour

225g (8oz) smoked haddock fillets,
   skinned
½ white onion, cut into rings
25g (1oz) unsalted butter
salt and freshly ground black pepper
1 bay leaf
150ml (5fl oz) fish stock
1 ripe avocado, stoned, peeled and
   chopped
1 tablespoon powdered gelatine
2 tablespoons white wine
7 tablespoons double cream
1 egg white
cucumber, tomato and red onion
   salad to serve (optional)

method

1 Place the fish in a shallow pan and top with the onion rings. Dot with the butter, season with pepper and add the bay leaf and stock. Poach for about 4 minutes until the fish flakes with a fork. Remove the fish, reserving the cooking liquid, and set aside to cool.

2 Remove the onion and bay leaf from the cooking liquid and boil until it has reduced by two thirds. Flake the fish into a food processor, add the cooking liquid and blend until smooth. Transfer the fish to a large bowl and stir in the chopped avocado.

3 In a small saucepan, sprinkle the gelatine over 2 tablespoons of cold water and leave until it becomes spongy. Add the wine and heat until it is completely dissolved, stirring continuously. Pour into the fish and mix in well.

4 Whip the cream in a bowl. In another bowl, beat the egg white with a little salt until stiff, then fold in the cream. Fold this mixture into the fish and season to taste. Pour either into individual ramekins or into a large dish, cover with cling film and leave in the fridge for at least 1 hour. Serve with cucumber, tomato and red onion salad if desired.

Alternative fish:
smoked mackerel

Oriental squid

This dish is one of my best sellers in Zilli Fish and very popular at the annual event La Dolce Vita and at Taste of London: people now phone to book their portion just to make sure we have enough for them!

SERVES: 4

Preparation time: 10 minutes
Cooking time: 4–5 minutes

1 tablespoon olive oil
3 teaspoons sesame oil
4 squid, cleaned and cut into rings (see page 44)
½ teaspoon finely chopped fresh root ginger
2 tablespoons chopped coriander
1 red chilli, seeded and finely chopped
3 spring onions, finely chopped
1 stalk lemongrass, finely chopped
2 tablespoons soy sauce

method

1 Heat the olive oil and sesame oil in a wok or large frying pan, add the squid and stir fry for about 2–3 minutes.

2 Mix together the ginger, coriander, chilli, spring onions, lemongrass and 1 teaspoon of soy sauce and add to the squid. Stir-fry for 1 minute until the herbs and squid are well mixed and hot. Stir in the rest of the soy sauce just before serving.

Alternative fish:
tiger prawns, cuttlefish

PREPARING SQUID

1 Rinse the squid thoroughly in cold water. The squid should not smell of fish at all; if it does, it is not fresh and should not be eaten.

2 Holding the body of the squid firmly in one hand, grasp the base of the tentacles and pull away from the body to remove the entrails.

3 Still holding onto the body, place your hand in the cavity of the squid and remove the 'plastic' backbone or quill.

4 Take a sharp knife and cut through the eyes on the tentacles.

5 Using both hands, turn the squid tentacles almost inside out.

6 Using your thumb, push through the bottom of the tentacles until the 'third' eye pops out. Discard this.

7 Firmly grasping the wings, push your fingers between the wings and body of the squid and pull. This will remove the wings and most of the skin.

8 Pull the remaining skin off the squid, making sure you end up with a clean, white body.

9 With a thumb or finger, make an indentation in the bottom of the squid. Remove your thumb and place a small carrot in this indentation.

10 Using the carrot, turn the squid inside out, remove the carrot and clean off any insides and membrane from the squid.

11 Using scissors or a sharp knife, cut off both ends of the squid, then cut along the natural indentation in the squid.

12 Place the squid with the whiter inside up on a board. Using a knife score it diagonally until you have a criss-cross pattern.

Grilled squid with sweet chilli sauce and rocket

This is my favourite way of cooking squid: the flavour of the squid can be lost in the oil when you fry it. Make sure that you don't overcook the squid or it will become tough. Scoring the inside of the squid helps it to cook evenly.

SERVES: 4

Preparation time: 10 minutes
Cooking time: 6 minutes

4 squid (350g/12oz each), cleaned
85ml (3fl oz) extra virgin olive oil
sea salt flakes and freshly ground
   black pepper
2 tablespoons balsamic vinegar
250g (9oz) wild rocket, washed and
   drained
lemon wedges to serve

Alternative fish:
octopus (cook for at least
6 minutes)

Chilli sauce
2 tablespoons nam pla (fish sauce)
2 tablespoons water
4 red chillies, finely chopped
juice of 1 lemon
1 teaspoon brown sugar

method

1 Using a thin knife, score the inside of the squid to form a criss-cross pattern (see step 12 opposite).

2 Heat a grill pan to medium-hot. Place the squid, scored side down, on the pan and brush with a little of the oil, then sprinkle with salt and pepper. Grill for 4–5 minutes, turn over, brush with more oil and season. Grill for a further 3–4 minutes until squid begins to curl up at the edges and is tender. Slice each in half.

3 Meanwhile make the chilli sauce: in a food processor, blend the fish sauce, water, chilli, lemon juice and sugar and process for about 2–3 minutes until the dressing is smooth .

4 Place the remainder of the olive oil and the balsamic vinegar in a screw-top jar and shake vigorously to combine. Season to taste. Place the rocket in a large bowl and pour over the oil and vinegar dressing. Distribute the rocket between 4 plates and arrange the hot squid on top. Spoon over the chilli sauce and serve with lemon wedges.

Squid and spicy Italian sausage stew

This particular recipe takes me back to my childhood when my mother used to cook this for the family quite often. She made her own sausages to give it that extra special taste. This recipe also works really well with octopus.

SERVES: 4

Preparation time: 20 minutes
Cooking time: 1 hour 30 minutes

900g potatoes, peeled and diced
1 tablespoon olive oil
2 garlic cloves, finely chopped
1 white onion, finely chopped
2 carrots, cut into small dices
2 leeks cut into small dices
70g frozen peas
1 fresh chilli, finely chopped

250ml stock
12 baby squid, cleaned and cut
   in half
600g spicy Italian sausage, cut
   into thick slices
1 glass (175ml) good red wine
1 teaspoon finely chopped rosemary
   2 whole bay leaves
1 tablespoon finely chopped parsley
sea salt and ground black pepper

method

1 Pan fry the garlic and onions in the olive oil for 3 minutes over a medium heat, making sure that the garlic doesn't burn.

2 Add the carrots, leeks, chilli, potatoes, squid and sausage and cook for a further 5 minutes, then add the red wine and let it completely reduce. Add the stock, bay leaves and rosemary and cook for 1 hour over a medium heat. Add the peas and cook for a further 20 minutes. Thicken with flour and season to taste, adding the parsley. Serve with some warm crusty bread.

Gluten-free linguine with squid and monkfish

Gluten-free for me used to be a no-go area but since I tried it I've changed my mind and especially with this sauce you will love this recipe, particularly if you don't want to eat too much pasta – what a great alternative. Any firm-fleshed fish will work with this recipe.

SERVES: 4

Preparation time: 15 minutes
Cooking time: 10 minutes

350g (12oz) monkfish cleaned, cut into chunks
100g (4oz) squid rings
175cl dry white wine such as Trebbiano

1 tablespoon extra virgin olive oil
½ a red chilli, finely chopped
8 spring onions, finely sliced
1 garlic clove, crushed
1 tablespoon fresh chopped basil leaves
1 jar passata
350g (12oz) gluten-free linguine
sea salt flakes and freshly ground black pepper
torn basil leaves to serve

method

1 Pan fry the spring onions, chilli and garlic in the olive oil for 1 minute and then remove the garlic clove.

2 Add the squid and cook for 2 minutes and then add the monkfish chunks. Pan fry for a further 2 minutes and then deglaze the pan with the white wine. After 2 minutes add the passata and chopped basil and leave to cook for 3 minutes.

3 Add the pasta to boiling salted water, gently easing into the water. Stir and return to a rolling boil. Cook the pasta according to pack instructions.

4 Drain the pasta and add to the saucepan with sauce and toss to combine. If the sauce is a little too thick, add some of the reserved pasta water. Serve immediately, garnishing with the remaining basil.

Dover sole

Plaice

Lemon sole

Halibut

Brill

Flat Fish

Turbot

Flat Fish

Flat fish are strange-looking creatures, most of which are found in the Atlantic. All species start life with an eye on each side of their head like round fish. At this stage they swim upright near the surface. As they mature, one eye moves around so that both eyes are on top of the head. This enables them to move along the sea bed, feeding on whatever passes by, while keeping a look out for predators. Flat fish also have the ability to change their colour to blend in with their surroundings. Because they do not have to chase their food – or flee predators – their flesh is always delicate and white without too much muscle and fibre. They have a simple bone structure, so even people nervous of bones can cope with them. The best way of eating most flat fish is pan fried with a little lemon, parsley and browned butter – stonger flavours will overpower the delicate flavour of these fish. The exceptions are plaice, which needs a bit more flavouring and is delicious cooked in breadcrumbs, and halibut, which is best cooked in a sauce to keep it moist. Good rich sauces for this fish include hollandaise, parsley and lobster.

BRILL *Schopthalmus rhombus* or *Rhombus laevis*
Brill is similar to turbot in both appearance and taste but is regarded as the poor relation, a reputation that is unjustified as it has a fine, softish white flesh with a delicate flavour. The top of the fish has dark grey skin with small scales and the underbelly is either creamy or a pinkish white.

DOVER SOLE *Solea solea* and *Solea vulgaris*
Widely regarded as the best fish of all, Dover sole has a firm, delicate flesh with a superb flavour. The Dover sole has a well-proportioned oval shape with a greyish or light brown skin and eyes on the righthand side of its head. Most Dover sole weigh between 200 and 600g (7oz to 1lb 5oz).

FLOUNDER *Platichthys flesus*
This famous saltwater fish, also known as fluke, is a dull brown-grey or green on its upper side with a white underbelly. Flounder is similar to plaice and, like plaice, is best eaten as soon as possible after being caught. It is often considered to be the 'fish for people who don't like fish' and is sought after by both anglers and restaurateurs. The best way to cook flounder is to either steam it or fry it.

HALIBUT *Hippoglossus hippoglossus*
The largest of all the flat fish – it can grow up to 2m (6½ft) in length and weigh more than 200kg (440lb) – the halibut is found in very cold, deep waters. It has an elongated, greenish brown body, pointed head, white underbelly and, as with most flat fish, eyes on the righthand side of its head. The flesh is fine, with a meaty texture and a delicious flavour.

LEMON SOLE *Microstomus kitt*
This fish is actually related to the dab, plaice and flounder and not, as you might expect, to the Dover sole. The lemon sole is oval in shape with smooth, reddish brown skin, a very small head and bulging eyes. Its flesh is soft and white and similar to that of plaice but of a superior quality. Lemon sole is an extremely good alternative to the more expensive Dover sole.

PLAICE *Pleuronectes platessa*
This is a very distinctive looking fish that has a smooth, dark greyish-brown skin with orange spots on the top and a completely white underbelly. As with most flat fish, the eyes are on the righthand side of the head. Plaice has a soft, white flesh that can be fairly bland in flavour. An average plaice weighs between 400g and 1kg (14oz and 2lb 4oz) and can live for up to 50 years.

SKATE *Rajus batis*
This flat seawater fish lives in cold and temperate waters on the bottom of the sea where its colouring – a grey or brown back with lighter spots and black dots – camouflages it on the sea bed. Skates lay eggs in rectangular cases with 'tassels' in each corner, which when washed up on the beach are known as 'mermaids' purses'. When alive, skates contain little ammonia, but after death they produce a lot more. The smell of ammonia should disappear when the skate is cooked; if it doesn't, the skate is not fresh.

TURBOT *Psetta maxima* and *Scophthalmus maximus*
While not the most attractive of fish, the turbot makes up for its strange appearance with its superb texture and taste; indeed, it is a very close contender to the Dover sole. The turbot has a very tough, warty flesh, a small head and a large body. Unlike other flat fish, its underbelly is sometimes grey. The flesh is creamy white, with a firm, dense texture and a lovely sweet flavour.

Mediterranean-style brill

I love brill: it is not a cheap fish but it has a great texture. This recipe reminds me of my early years of cooking fish and is simplicity at its best.

Alternative fish:
sole, plaice

SERVES: 4

Preparation time: 10 minutes
Cooking time: 25 minutes

4 brill (300g/10½oz each), cleaned
4 garlic cloves
100g (3½oz) black olives
400g (14oz) cherry tomatoes
2 tablespoons shredded basil
4 fresh anchovies in oil, drained
1 tablespoon capers
5 tablespoons extra virgin
  olive oil
5 tablespoons white wine
1 tablespoon chopped fresh
  parsley

method

1 Preheat the oven to 190°C (375°F/gas 5). Rinse the fish under cold running water and with a sharp knife slash the skin of each fish a few times on both sides.

2 Place the fish in a roasting pan with the garlic, olives, cherry tomatoes, 1 tablespoon of basil, anchovies, capers and olive oil and cook in the oven for 15 minutes.

3 Add the white wine to the roasting pan and cook for a further 10 minutes.

4 Remove from the oven and serve sprinkled with chopped fresh parsley and the remainder of the shredded basil.

Skate with black butter

These skate wings are fried, but you can also roast them. If you do so, watch the edges as they tend to burn. Cover them with foil and the skate will cook quite quickly.

SERVES: 4

Preparation time: 5 minutes plus 1 hour soaking time
Cooking time: 15 minutes

4 skate wings (225g/8oz each)
4 tablespoons red wine vinegar
8 tablespoons seasoned flour
olive oil for frying
salt and freshly ground black pepper
2 tablespoons chopped fresh parsley
150g (5½oz) butter
2 tablespoons drained capers

Alternative fish:
Dover sole, flounder, dab

method

1 Put the skate in a large shallow dish, cover with water and add a pinch of salt and a tablespoon of the vinegar. Leave to soak for 1 hour to remove any impurities, then rinse.

2 Dip the skate wings in the flour and then pan fry them in some olive oil, turning them occasionally, for about 15 minutes, depending on the size of the wings.

3 Remove the skate to a warm serving dish, season with salt and pepper and scatter parsley over.

4 Meanwhile, in a small pan, heat the butter until it foams and turns a rich brown colour. Add the capers and warm through, then pour over the skate and serve immediately.

Dover sole with peas and tomato sauce

What puzzles me about this fish is that it is local to the UK yet is always so expensive. Dover sole also tastes great simply grilled or roasted and served with lemon oil dressing.

SERVES: 4

Preparation time: 5 minutes
Cooking time: 35 minutes

6 tablespoons olive oil
1 red onion, finely chopped
3 garlic cloves, crushed
3 tablespoons Italian flat-leaf parsley
pinch of fennel seeds
1 glass dry white wine
400g (14oz) can chopped tomatoes or passata
salt and freshly ground black pepper
350g (12oz) shelled peas
4 whole Dover sole (400g/14oz each)
55g (2oz) butter

method

1 Heat 4 tablespoons of oil in a pan and add the onion, garlic, parsley and fennel seeds. Cook until the onions are translucent. Remove the garlic at this stage.

2 Add the wine to the pan and cook until it has evaporated, then add the tomatoes or passata and cook over a medium heat for 8 minutes until the sauce begins to thicken. Add salt and pepper and peas and cook over a low heat for 12 minutes.

3 Pan fry the Dover sole in 2 tablespoons of olive oil for 10 minutes on each side. Just before they are cooked, add the butter to the pan. Serve the fish with the tomato and pea sauce.

Alternative fish:
plaice, lemon sole

Right: Skate with black butter

1 You can obtain 4 fillets from a flat fish but they will not be identical in size because of the irregular shape of the fish.

2 Using a sharp knife or pair of scissors, remove the fins from either side of the fish's body.

3 Cut across the base of the tail with a sharp knife until you reach the bone.

4 Grip the fish firmly by the tail with one hand and with your other hand pull the skin away from you and off the fish.

Dover sole fillets Dijon

When I was working in the South of France this dish was regularly featured on the menu and was always extremely popular, so I am now sharing it with you.

SERVES: 4

Preparation time: 10 minutes
Cooking time: 30 minutes

25g (1oz) butter
2 tablespoons extra virgin olive oil
4 Dover sole fillets (200g/7oz each) or 4 whole Dover sole (400g/ 14oz each)

Shrimp sauce
25g (1oz) unsalted butter
1 tablespoon olive oil
1 garlic clove, crushed
150g (5½oz) shrimp in brine or small raw tiger prawns
4 tablespoons white wine
190ml (6½fl oz) cream
1 tablespoon chopped dill
1 tablespoon Dijon mustard
1 tablespoon lemon juice
salt and freshly ground black pepper
spinach with celery and red peppers to serve (optional)

method

1 Heat the butter and oil in a pan, then add the fish and cook over a medium heat for about 6 minutes on each side until golden brown and cooked through. Transfer to a warm oven until the sauce is ready.

2 To make the sauce: melt the butter and oil in a pan and add the crushed garlic. Cook gently for 1 minute until the garlic is golden then remove it from the pan. (Be careful not to burn the garlic as this will ruin the sauce.)

3 Add the shrimp to the pan and cook for 3 minutes or until they change to a nice pink colour. Add the wine and cook until almost completely evaporated, then stir in the cream, dill, mustard and lemon juice, warm through and season to taste. Serve sauce with the fish, with spinach, celery and red peppers if desired.

Alternative fish:
lemon sole, halibut, plaice

5 Pull the roe out of the fish; it should come away in one long piece.

6 Using a sharp knife and starting from the head, cut down the back bone of the fish. Then lay the knife as close to the bone as you can.

7 Cut down towards the tail using long stroking movements to remove the first fillet. Repeat this process for the other 3 fillets.

Lemon sole rolls stuffed with leeks, carrots and prawns

Lemon sole fillets are one of the specialities of my restaurant and well liked by my customers. If you love sole, this is the recipe for you – simple and fantastic.

SERVES: 4

Preparation time: 10 minutes
Cooking time: 25 minutes

3 carrots, grated
1 leek, grated or finely chopped
5 tablespoons breadcrumbs
150g (5½oz) finely chopped prawns
1 tablespoon lemon juice
salt and freshly ground black pepper
6 lemon sole fillets (250g/9oz each)
1 tablespoon olive oil
lemon oil
grilled Portobello mushrooms and
    sautéed red cabbage to serve
    (optional)

Alternative fish:
plaice, brill, Dover sole

method

1 Preheat the oven to 200°C (400°F/gas 6).

2 In a bowl mix together the carrots, leek, breadcrumbs and prawns. Add the lemon juice and season with salt and pepper.

3 Lay the fish fillets skin side up (make sure this is the white skin and not the spotted/dark skin) on a board. Place one quarter of the filling near the end of one fillet and, using your fingers to ensure the filling stays in place, carefully roll up the fillet to make a round parcel. Repeat with remaining lemon sole fillets and filling.

4 Place the rolls on a baking tray and sprinkle with olive oil. Cover with aluminium foil and cook in the oven for 25 minutes.

5 Serve the lemon sole rolls drizzled with lemon oil and on a bed of grilled Portobello mushrooms and sautéed red cabbage if desired.

1 Lay a piece of parchment paper on a board and place fish and other ingredients in the centre. Fold up all edges to make a parcel.

Lemon sole in parchment

I love the fact that this recipe contains lots of vegetables! Try to include a variety of seasonal vegetables in the parcel – any combination will work.

SERVES: 4

Preparation time: 15 minutes
Cooking time: 10 minutes

2 carrots, cut into thin strips
2 courgettes, cut into thin strips
2 leeks, cut into thin strips
1 fennel bulb, cut into thin strips
1 green pepper, cut into thin strips
2 tomatoes, peeled, seeded and
    diced
salt and freshly ground black pepper
2 tablespoons chopped fresh
    tarragon
4 lemon sole fillets (200g/7oz
    each), cut in half, or 8 fillets
    if quite small
3 tablespoons olive oil
4 tablespoons Champagne or
    sparkling wine

Alternative fish:
haddock, scallops, halibut

method

1 Preheat the oven to 190°C (375°F/gas 5). Cut 4 pieces of non-stick baking parchment or rice paper about 45cm (18in) square, fold each piece in half and, using the fold as the centre line, cut out a half heart shape.

2 Open the paper hearts and distribute the carrot, courgette, leek, fennel and pepper strips and the diced tomatoes between them, placing them in the fold of each heart. Sprinkle the vegetables with salt and pepper and half the tarragon. Arrange 2 pieces of fish over each bed. Sprinkle with the remaining tarragon, the olive oil and wine.

3 Fold the top half of the paper heart over the fish and vegetables, fold the edges over and twist and roll the paper to form an airtight parcel.

4 Put the parcels onto a baking tray and bake in the oven for 10 minutes, or until the paper is brown and well puffed out. Serve the fish and vegetables still in their parchment parcels.

Turbot with beetroot and potato rosti

Turbot fillet is excellent but if you manage to get a fresh whole fish then a fantastic way to cook it is roasted with thyme and garlic.

SERVES: 4

Preparation time: 15 minutes
Cooking time: 45 minutes

4 x 200g turbot fillets
1 tablespoon extra virgin olive oil
300g Maris Piper potatoes, skin on
2 beetroot, peeled
1 teaspoon chives, finely chopped
2 whole red peppers
sea salt and ground black pepper

method

1 Cook the potatoes in boiling water for 8 minutes, drain and set aside to cool. Peel and grate the potatoes. Place the whole peppers on a baking tray, sprinkle with sea salt and cook in a 180°C oven for 45 minutes. Remove and place in a bowl covered with cling film. Once the peppers are cool, remove the skin and seeds and blend in a food processor.

2 Grate the beetroot into the same bowl as the potato, add the chives and season with sea salt and ground black pepper. Mix together well.

3 Make 4 rostis by shaping them in the egg ring. Place onto a greased baking tray and cook for 20 minutes in a 180°C oven until cooked through.

4 Meanwhile pan fry the turbot in the olive oil for 5 minutes skin side down, place the pan in the same oven and cook for a further 10 minutes. Remove and serve on top of the rosti with a drizzle of extra virgin olive oil.

Alternative fish:
halibut or tuna

Halibut with saffron sauce and stewed leeks

If available, halibut is a great fish for this recipe and the leeks work much better with it than onions. The soft, lighter flavour of the leeks really complements this fish: anything too heavy would kill the fish's delicate flavour.

SERVES: 4

Preparation time: 10 minutes
Cooking time: 25 minutes

4 halibut fillets (175g/6oz each)
2 pinches of saffron
400ml (14fl oz) fish stock
200ml (7fl oz) white wine
200g (7oz) leeks, cut into 10cm
   (4in) lengths
55g (2oz) butter
salt and freshly ground black pepper
1 teaspoon lemon juice
chopped spring onions to serve

method

1 Preheat the oven to 190°C (375°F/gas 5).

2 Place the fish in an ovenproof dish, season, add saffron and pour over fish stock and wine. Poach in the oven for 8 minutes.

3 Drain the liquid from the dish into a saucepan and add the leeks. Keep the fish warm. Cook the leeks gently until soft, about 15 minutes. Add the butter, seasoning and lemon juice and stir until butter has melted.

4 Remove leeks with a slotted spoon and divide between 4 plates, place fish on top and pour saffron sauce over. Sprinkle with chopped spring onions and serve.

Alternative fish:
turbot, monkfish, cod, salmon

Flounder with grapes, sultanas and balsamic vinegar

The inspiration for this recipe came when I was on holiday in South Africa, where they tend to marry fish with fruit a lot. The sweetness of the fruit is offset by the sharpness of the balsamic vinegar. This is a really light, well-balanced dish, which tastes particularly fine when served with a rocket salad.

SERVES: 4

Preparation time: 10 minutes
Cooking time: 15 minutes

4 flounder fillets (175g/6oz each)
salt and freshly ground black pepper
juice of 1 lemon
25g (1oz) butter
85g (3oz) sultanas
175g (6oz) seedless grapes
2 tablespoons freshly chopped
   parsley
3 tablespoons balsamic vinegar
5 tablespoons marsala wine

method

1 Preheat the oven to 200°C (400°F/gas 6). Arrange the fish in a shallow baking dish, sprinkle with salt, pepper and lemon juice and dot with the butter.

2 In a bowl, stir together the sultanas, grapes, parsley, balsamic vinegar and marsala wine. Spoon a quarter of this mixture over each fillet and bake in the oven for 15 minutes.

Alternative fish:
salmon, sea bass, turbot

Right: Flounder with grapes, sultanas and balsamic vinegar

Halibut with lemon, red onion and coriander

I have tested this recipe over and over again with my customers and it's always a winner.
Don't forget to add plenty of coriander – what a great herb!

SERVES: 4

Preparation time: 10 minutes plus
  1 hour marinating time
Cooking time: 15 minutes

juice of 1 lemon
1 teaspoon chopped garlic
1 teaspoon paprika
1 teaspoon ground cumin
1 teaspoon chopped fresh tarragon
salt and freshly ground black pepper
4 halibut steaks (175g/6oz each)
4 tablespoons extra virgin olive oil
100g (3½oz) flour
275ml (9½fl oz) fish or vegetable
  stock
1 chilli, seeded and chopped
3 tablespoons chopped coriander
1 red onion, sliced

method

1 Mix the lemon juice, garlic, paprika, cumin, tarragon and some salt and pepper together in a bowl. Place the halibut in a dish and spoon over this lemon mix. Set aside to marinate for 1 hour.

2 Heat 3 tablespoons of olive oil in a pan. Dust the fish with flour, add to the pan and cook over a gentle heat for 3 minutes on one side, then turn the fish over and fry on the other side for a further 2 minutes. Pour over the stock, cover and simmer for 5 minutes. Add the chilli and half the coriander to the pan and cook for a further 5 minutes. Transfer to a serving dish.

3 Meanwhile heat the remaining olive oil in a separate pan and fry the onion until soft. Scatter the fried onion over the fish with the remaining coriander.

Alternative fish:
turbot, sea bass, cod

Turbot hollandaise

This is a very special fish so it deserves a special sauce. A lot of people are nervous about making hollandaise, but it is really very easy and well worth making the effort. This is a great dinner party recipe – simple yet elegant.

SERVES: 4

Preparation time: 10 minutes
Cooking time: 10 minutes

2 tablespoons extra virgin olive oil
4 turbot fillets (175g/6oz each)
1 tablespoon chopped fresh parsley
steamed asparagus spears to serve
    (optional)

Hollandaise sauce
115g (4oz) unsalted butter
1–2 tablespoons lemon juice
2 egg yolks
salt and ground white pepper

method

1 First make the hollandaise sauce: melt the butter in a pan. In a heatproof bowl, mix together the lemon juice and egg yolks. Add salt and pepper and whisk until completely smooth.

2 Place the bowl over a pan of simmering water and slowly pour the melted butter onto the egg-yolk mixture in a steady stream, beating continuously with a wooden spoon to make a smooth, creamy sauce. Add more lemon juice to taste if necessary.

3 Heat the olive oil in a pan until hot, then add the turbot fillets and pan fry for 2–3 minutes on each side until cooked through and golden.

4 Serve the fish with the hollandaise poured over and sprinkled with parsley. If necessary you can rehydrate the hollandaise with some warm water. For presentation you could place the dish under a hot grill so that the hollandaise browns a touch. Serve with asparagus spears, if desired.

Alternative fish:
swordfish, salmon, sea bass

BREADING SOLE OR OTHER FISH FILLETS

1 Place beaten egg in one shallow dish, flour in another and breadcrumbs in a third. Have your fish fillets ready to dip.

2 Dip each fish fillet in the flour first; this will ensure that the rest of the ingredients stick to the fish.

3 Then dip the fillet into the beaten egg. Make sure it is well covered in egg or the breadcrumbs will not adhere to the fish.

4 Finally place the fillet in the breadcrumbs. Pat the fish down gently with your fingers to ensure it is evenly coated. Turn it over and repeat.

Fried lemon sole with tomato sauce

I love eating fish in breadcrumbs and lemon sole is perfect for this recipe: the crispness of the breadcrumbs with the flavoursome tomato sauce is a great combination.

SERVES: 4

Preparation time: 15 minutes
Cooking time: 1 hour 10 minutes

25g (1oz) plain flour
2 eggs, beaten
85g (3oz) breadcrumbs
4 lemon sole fillets (200g/7oz each)
15g (½oz) butter
1 tablespoon olive oil
1 lemon, cut into wedges, to serve
minted new potatoes to serve

Tomato sauce
2 tablespoons extra virgin olive oil
2 shallots, finely diced
1 garlic clove, finely diced
400g (14oz) can chopped tomatoes
   or passata
8 black olives, cut in half
salt and freshly ground black pepper
1 branch fresh basil leaves

method

1 To make the tomato sauce, heat the olive oil in a large pan, add the shallots and garlic and cook for about 6 minutes over a low heat. Stir in the tomatoes and simmer, uncovered, for 40 minutes, stirring occasionally. Add olives and cook for a further 5 minutes. Season to taste, tear the basil leaves and add to the sauce.

2 Spread the flour on a plate and pour the egg mixture into a dish; place the breadcrumbs on another plate. Dip the sole in the flour, then the egg and then the breadcrumbs, making sure it is well coated.

3 Heat the butter and olive oil in a pan and pan fry the sole for 4 minutes on each side until a lovely golden brown.

4 Drain the fish and serve with lemon wedges, tomato sauce and minted new potatoes.

Alternative fish:
plaice, brill, John Dory

Plaice goujons in sparkling wine batter

Plaice is perfect for this recipe as it has a good firm texture so holds together well. Plaice is not normally regarded as being very special, but I happen to disagree: it is extremely versatile and ranks up there with Dover sole for me.

SERVES: 4

Preparation time: 25 minutes plus 1 hour resting time for batter
Cooking time: 5 minutes

85g (3oz) self-raising flour
55g (2oz) cornflour
1 teaspoon salt
1 egg white
250ml (9fl oz) Champagne
seasoned flour for coating
700g (1lb 8oz) plaice fillets, cut into goujons
vegetable oil for deep frying
tartar sauce to serve (optional)

Alternative fish:
codling, cod, lemon sole

method

1 In a bowl, combine the flour, cornflour, salt and egg white. Whisk in the Champagne until you have a smooth batter. Leave in the fridge to rest for at least 1 hour.

2 Place some seasoned flour in a shallow dish and dip the goujons into the flour to coat evenly, then dip them into the batter.

3 Heat the vegetable oil in a large pan. Drop the coated goujons directly into the hot oil and cook until crispy and golden brown. Remove goujons from the oil with a slotted spoon and drain on paper towels. Serve immediately, with tartar sauce if desired.

Brown trout

Rainbow trout

Sea trout

Eel

Mackerel

Herring

Oily Fish

Sardine

Anchovies

Whitebait

Salmon

Oily Fish

Oily fish are generally very popular as they are cheap, healthy and readily available. Oily fish are good for the brain and great at helping to prevent heart attacks and strokes; they can also help make your skin look younger. They are a great source of protein, rich in magnesium, zinc, selenium and vitamin A, plus B vitamins, and – most importantly – they are a good source of omega 3 fatty acids, which make the blood less 'sticky', thus helping to reduce the risk of blood clots that could cause heart attacks. It is a well known fact that people who eat a lot of oily fish, like the Japanese, tend to live longer and have the lowest rates of heart disease. Most oily fish, such as sardines, mackerel, herrings, are quite 'fishy' fish, but don't be put off: I think they are the way forward in healthy eating. But aside from all their many healthy benefits, the best thing about oily fish is that they happen to be very good eating. They tend to have no scales so are easy to prepare and for me there is nothing better than a fresh mackerel simply cooked on the grill with lemon and butter – a wonderful lunch or dinner.

ANCHOVY *Engraulis encrasilcolus*
This small fish prefers the warm waters of the Mediterranean. There are various species to be found all round the world, but it is normally about 20cm (8in) long with a green/blue back and a silvery belly. Anchovies are mostly sold canned or bottled in oil; fresh ones are rare.

EEL genus *Anguilla*
Eels could be considered to be marine fish rather than freshwater ones. They start and end their life in the sea, but spend most of their life in fresh water, and this is where they tend to be caught. Eels will live out of water for a long time and then keep well even after death. If you buy live eels, they need to be killed, bled, skinned, cleaned and cut. This is a very long and complicated process so I recommend that you ask your fishmonger to do it for you. Eels are relatively fatty fish and make a rich dish.

HERRING *Clupea harengus*
This fish has a dark blue-black back, shading down to silvery white on its belly. An adult herring is about 20–25cm (8–10in) long. The flesh is fairly fat and for this reason, herrings lend themselves to being pickled.

MACKEREL *Scomber scombrus*
Mackerel are very easy to identify because of their beautiful greeny-blue skin with wavy bands of black, and green backs with silvery bellies. I love mackerel when they are fresh and in their prime, which is normally in late spring and early summer. Mackerel, like most oily fish, is very high in omega 3 oils.

SALMON *Salmo salar*
One of the most widely available and popular fish to be found in markets and supermarkets. Almost all salmon sold is farmed and tends to have firm, pink flesh with not too much fat. Wild salmon, which is available at a higher price, has firmer, deeper pink flesh.

SARDINES *Sardina pilchardus* and *Clupea pilchardus*
Most people assume that sardines and pilchards are different fish. In fact they are not: a pilchard is just a larger sardine. Sardines owe their name to Sardinia, where they were once found in large quantities. Sardines need to be very fresh to be at their best: stay away from any damaged, dull-looking sardines as they will not be great eating. If you want to stuff them, then make sure you choose larger sardines, which will hold together better when you are filling them.

SWORDFISH *Xiphias gladius*
Aptly named after its swordlike nose, which acounts for a third of the size of the fish, the swordfish can be found in all the great oceans. Swordfish have a firm white flesh, which is perfect for steaks.

TROUT
This is the most well known of the freshwater fish and is very popular with fishermen. There are two main types of freshwater trout: rainbow (*Salmo gairdneri*) and brown trout (*Salmo trutta*), both of which can be caught in the wild. However, most commercially available trout have been farmed. Hatchery rainbow trout are fed a caryatid pigment to give them pink flesh; wild rainbow trout have a moist white flesh. Sea trout (also *Salmo trutta*) is similar to salmon in that it is migratory and eats crustaceans that contain the caryatid pigment, which gives the fish its distinctive pink colour. Be careful when ordering trout in the southern states of the USA as what is known elsewhere as croaker is called sea trout or trout there.

TUNA genus *Thunnus*
These torpedo-shaped fish have powerful muscles and a firm, dark, meaty flesh. They gather in shoals and migrate towards the shore when breeding where they are then caught in huge numbers by enormous drift-nets. Unfortunately, these nets can also catch dolphin, turtles and other marine life; 'dolphin-friendly' canned tuna has not been caught by drift-net. As with many other popular fish, over fishing is leading to a decline in tuna stocks around the world. The finest of all tuna, bluefin, is normally used for sushi and sashimi and is highly prized in Japan. Bluefin tuna, which is also the largest of the tuna family, has a deep red flesh. Any tuna that has changed to a light brown colour should be discarded as this means it is past its prime.

WHITEBAIT
Whitebait is not a species of fish but rather the term used to group any tiny fish – typically 'bait' are only 25–50mm (1–2in) in length. They may be young sprats or herrings or other small fish. Because of their small size, there is no cleaning involved – you eat the entire fish, including head, fins and gut – but whitebait is very tender and edible.

Mackerel with mustard and lemon butter

This is one of the best ways of cooking mackerel – simple and full of flavour. You can use fillets instead of whole mackerel if you wish: you won't need to score the flesh and they'll need cooking for about 3 minutes on each side.

SERVES: 4

Preparation time: 10 minutes
Cooking time: 20 minutes

4 fresh mackerel (175g/6oz each), cleaned
salt and freshly ground black pepper
4 slices lemon
4 sprigs rosemary
115g (4oz) butter, melted
grated zest of 1 lemon
2 tablespoons lemon juice
2 tablespoons wholegrain mustard
3 tablespoons chopped fresh parsley
225g (8oz) baby spinach

method

1 Preheat the grill. Make 3 slashes into the skin of the fish on either side, then season with salt and pepper. Insert a slice of lemon and a sprig of rosemary into the cavity of each fish.

2 In a bowl, mix together the melted butter, lemon zest and juice, mustard and parsley; season.

3 Place the mackerel on a grill rack and brush with the mustard butter. Grill for about 10 minutes on each side, occasionally brushing with more butter.

4 Arrange the baby spinach on 4 plates and place a mackerel on top of each. Heat the remaining mustard butter until bubbling and pour over the fish before serving.

Alternative fish:
sardines, herring

CLEANING AND FILLETING MACKEREL

1 Using scissors or a knife, make an incision in the belly towards the tail and cut upwards. Pull out innards and wash the fish in cold water.

2 Using scissors, cut off all the fins. Smooth fish such as mackerel and trout do not need scaling.

3 Insert the edge of a sharp knife by the gills and press down to make an incision.

4 Keeping the knife close to the backbone, cut towards the tail and remove the fillet. Repeat on the other side so you have 2 fillets.

Mackerel Californian style

This recipe is also referred to as blackened and can be done with Cajun spice. Mackerel is a well-known fish but not very popular and I don't know why: it's delicious and, as a bonus, it's good for you – it's full of omega oils.

SERVES: 4

Preparation time: 10 minutes
Cooking time: 8 minutes

2 teaspoons paprika
1½ teaspoons salt
½ teaspoon onion powder
½ teaspoon garlic powder
½ teaspoon white pepper
½ teaspoon black pepper
½ teaspoon dried dill
½ teaspoon dried oregano
2 large mackerel (500g/1lb 2oz each), cleaned and filleted
115g (4oz) butter
fresh oregano sprigs
lemon slices
roasted leeks to serve (optional)

method

1 Mix together the paprika, salt, onion powder, garlic powder, white and black pepper and dried dill and oregano in a small bowl. Sprinkle this spice mixture over each fillet until well coated.

2 Heat half the butter in a heavy-based frying pan until very hot, add 2 of the fish fillets and cook over a medium heat for about 2 minutes on each side. Remove immediately, cover and keep warm. Add the remaining butter to the pan and cook the other fillets.

3 Transfer the fish to serving plates and garnish with oregano sprigs and lemon slices. Serve with the remaining butter from the pan poured around and accompanied by roasted leeks, if desired.

Alternative fish:
red snapper, tuna, salmon
(make sure they are thick cuts)

CLEANING AND FILLETING SALMON

1 Using the back of a knife and working from the tail to the head, scrape the fish to remove all the scales. Wash the fish under cold water.

2 Using a sharp knife, lift the gill and make a diagonal cut behind through to the backbone.

3 Keeping the knife as close to the backbone as possible, cut towards the tail, lifting the fillet as you go.

4 Run your fingers down the fillet and, using a pair of tweezers or pliers, remove the pin bones all down the fillet.

SALMON PARCEL

1 With a sharp knife, make a horizontal incision in the centre of the steak. Cut across to form a pocket in the middle of the steak.

2 Carefully open up the pocket in the steak with your fingers, ready to insert the stuffing.

Salmon stuffed with crab and spinach with dill sauce

This dish is incredibly popular with my customers. It's a very easy recipe that looks fantastic on the plate, so if you want to impress your friends, give this a try.

SERVES: 4

Preparation time: 15 minutes
Cooking time: 12 minutes

4 salmon fillets (185g/6½oz each)
100g (3½oz) fresh crab meat
200g (7oz) fresh spinach, sautéed
    and finely chopped
1 garlic clove, finely chopped
500ml (18fl oz) full-fat milk
1 teaspoon soy sauce
25g (1oz) fresh dill, chopped
lightly steamed mangetout to serve
    (optional)
dill sprigs to garnish

Alternative fish:
salmon trout, halibut, turbot

method

1 Preheat the oven to 180°C (350°F/gas 4).

2 Using a sharp knife, cut a small pocket into the middle of each salmon fillet. In a bowl, mix together the crab meat, spinach and garlic and stuff into each salmon fillet.

3 Place a large piece of aluminium foil in a roasting pan so that the edges come up the sides of the pan. Place all the fillets in the centre of the foil, leaving 1cm (½in) between each one.

4 In a jug, stir together the milk, soy sauce and dill. Pour over the salmon fillets. Fold over the edges of the foil to enclose the fish and pinch together at the top to form a parcel. Cook in the oven for 10–12 minutes. Be careful not to overcook the salmon: it should be pink on the inside.

5 Serve the salmon hot, on a bed of mangetout if desired, with a little of the sauce on top. Garnish with fresh dill sprigs.

Swordfish paillard on Caesar salad

The firm flesh of swordfish lends itself brilliantly to this simple dish. In my mind, this is one of the best recipes in the book and my customers at Zilli Fish seem to agree!

Alternative fish:
tuna, monkfish

SERVES: 4

Preparation time: 15 minutes plus
 30 minutes marinating time
Cooking time: 12 minutes

4 swordfish steaks (175–200g/
 6–7oz each)
3 tablespoons extra virgin olive oil
juice of ½ lemon
1 teaspoon sea salt
2 baby cos lettuce, washed and
 leaves separated
150g (5½oz) herb croutons
75g (2½oz) grated Parmesan
55g (2oz) shaved Parmesan

Caesar dressing
1 egg
2 garlic cloves
3–4 fresh anchovy fillets
 (if canned, use only 2)
2 tablespoons lemon juice
125ml (4½fl oz) extra
 virgin olive oil

method

1 Marinate the swordfish in the olive oil, lemon juice and sea salt for at least half an hour.

2 Make the Caesar dressing by blending in a food processor the egg, garlic, anchovies and lemon juice. Then, in a steady stream, as if you were making mayonnaise, add the olive oil until the mixture thickens. Store in the fridge (for a maximum of 2 days) until ready to use.

3 Using some of the fish marinade, cook the swordfish in a griddle pan for 5–6 minutes on each side (depending on the thickness of the steak). The fish should be cooked but not cooked through, as it will continue to cook while on the plate.

4 In a bowl, mix together the lettuce, croutons, grated Parmesan and Caesar dressing. Combine well so that the dressing is evenly distributed.

5 Serve the swordfish on top the Caesar salad with the shaved Parmesan on top of the fish. Drizzle with a little of the marinade to serve.

Salmon with bok choi and soy sauce

If you can buy wild salmon – it has a very short season, only 8 weeks in February/March, and is quite expensive in comparison to farmed – it will be worth it as the flavour is amazing and will make a dish like this one a sure winner.

SERVES: 4

Preparation time: 10 minutes
Cooking time: 1 hour 40 minutes

1 leek, chopped
2 carrots chopped
½ onion
2 bay leaves
4 black peppercorns
4 salmon fillets (150–175g/
   5½–6oz each)
½ lemon
8 bok choi heads, blanched
soy sauce to serve

Alternative fish:
trout, sea bass

method

1 First make the broth that you are going to steam the salmon over. Fill a large pot with boiling water and add the leek, carrots, onion, bay leaves and peppercorns and boil for 1½ hours until the vegetables are soft.

2 Add the salmon to a steamer above the broth, top with the ½ lemon, cover and cook for 7–8 minutes. Add the blanched bok choi and cook for a further 1 minute. Remove the bok choi and the salmon and place on plate, season with soy sauce and serve.

Barbecued salmon with potato salad

This is not only a summer recipe – you could also cook the salmon on a simple griddle pan or even roast it. The Cajun spice really brings this dish together.

1 Hold the salmon firmly at the tail end and, with a sharp knife, slice through the fish in one movement. Cut steaks about 4cm (1½in) thick.

SERVES: 4

Preparation time: 10 minutes plus
   1 hour marinating time
Cooking time: 8–10 minutes

4 tablespoons extra virgin olive oil
1 tablespoon Cajun spice
1 teaspoon ground ginger
1 teaspoon cayenne pepper
1 tablespoon soy sauce
salt and freshly ground black pepper
4 salmon steaks (250g/9oz each)
500g (1lb 2oz) new potatoes, boiled
2 eggs, hard boiled
1 small red onion, finely chopped
3 tablespoons chopped parsley
6 tablepoons mayonnaise

method

1 Mix together the oil, Cajun spice, ginger, cayenne, soy sauce and black pepper in a bowl. Place the salmon in a shallow dish and pour this marinade over. Cover and leave in the fridge for 1 hour, turning occasionally.

2 Cut the potatoes in half, roughly chop the eggs and mix together with the red onion, parsley and mayonnaise. Season to taste and leave in the fridge until ready to use.

3 Heat the barbecue. Remove the salmon steaks from the marinade and place them on the grill. Cook for 3–4 minutes, basting with marinade. Turn over and repeat on the other side.

4 Remove and serve with the potato salad.

Alternative fish:
cod, tuna, swordfish

Sea trout and noodle salad

Any trout can be used for this recipe. I chose sea trout because the colour of the fish looks great on the plate with the noodles. For anyone on a budget, trout is the way forward – and it is as healthy as mackerel or sardines.

SERVES: 4

Preparation time: 10 minutes plus
   45 minutes marinating time
Cooking time: 8 minutes

4 sea trout fillets (200g/7oz each)
2 tablespoons soy sauce
2 tablespoons sake
4 tablespoons mirin
1 teaspoon soft brown sugar
2 teaspoons grated fresh root ginger
3 garlic cloves
2 tablespoons peanut oil
225g (8oz) noodles, cooked
55g (2oz) bean sprouts
2 tablespoons toasted seasame seeds
1 tablespoon chopped coriander

method

1 Place the trout fillets in a shallow dish. Mix together the soy sauce, sake, mirin, sugar, ginger and 1 crushed garlic clove. Pour this over the trout, making sure the fish is well coated by turning it in the marinade. Cover with cling film and leave in the fridge to marinate for at least 45 minutes.

2 Preheat the grill. Remove the trout from the dish, reserving the marinade, and place it on a baking sheet. Cook under the grill for 2–3 minutes (without turning it).

3 Heat the oil in a large heavy frying pan. Slice the 2 remaining cloves of garlic and add to the pan; cook until brown but do not allow to burn. Add the noodles and the marinade and cook for 3–4 minutes, stirring constantly. The marinade will reduce and coat the noodles in a syrupy glaze.

4 Add the bean sprouts and remove from the heat. Toss the noodles and transfer to a serving dish, top with the sea trout and sprinkle with sesame seeds and coriander before serving.

Alternative fish:
rainbow trout, salmon, swordfish

Right: Sea trout and noodle salad

1 Take several sheets of newspaper and dip them into a bowl of water. Make sure that you wet the whole paper thoroughly.

2 Carefully lay the newspaper on a board and place the fish on top. Lift one side of the paper and roll the fish up.

3 Place on a barbecue and cook. The paper will not burn but rather become hard; turn once. Gently start to open the parcel.

4 When you pull the paper away from the fish, the skin will come off with it. Do not eat the skin because of the dye from the paper.

Trout wrapped in newspaper

When I visited my friend at his house in Italy and saw a newspaper parcel on the barbecue, I thought I was seeing things. He told me about this recipe and I couldn't resist including it in this book. Don't be worried about the paper catching fire – it won't. Rather, it turns into a hard shell-like casing, which adds a smoky flavour to the fish.

SERVES: 4

Preparation time: 15 minutes
Cooking time: 20 minutes

4 trout (450g/1lb each), cleaned
4 sprigs fresh thyme
2 garlic cloves, sliced in half
1 tablespoon extra virgin olive oil
3 tablespoons lemon juice
salt and freshly ground black pepper
newspaper
chopped parsley
lemon wedges to serve
rocket and spinach salad with olive
    oil and balsamic vinegar dressing
    to serve

method

1 Stuff each trout with a sprig of thyme and half a clove of garlic. Brush with olive oil and then sprinkle with lemon juice. Season with salt and pepper.

2 Take the newspaper and wet it, then wrap each fish individually. Place on a barbecue and cook for 20 minutes, turning the parcels occasionally.

3 Remove from the grill and pull the paper off the fish; the skin will come off with the paper leaving you with just the flesh. Sprinkle with chopped parsely and serve with lemon wedges and a rocket and spinach salad with extra virgin olive oil and balsamic vinegar.

Alternative fish:
sea bass, snapper, salmon

Baked stuffed sardines

I love stuffed sardines and tend to eat them every time I am in Italy. Be careful not to over stuff the sardines, as not only will the fish split but they will also take a lot longer to cook.

Alternative fish:

herring, mackerel, trout

SERVES: 4

Preparation time: 25 minutes
Cooking time: 30 minutes

1 tablespoon olive oil
1 onion, finely chopped
1 garlic clove, crushed
85g (3oz) fresh breadcrumbs
1 tablespoon wholegrain mustard
2 tablespoons chopped parsley
1 egg yolk
2 tablespoons ricotta cheese
juice of 3 lemons and zest of 1
salt and freshly ground black pepper
12 fresh sardines, cleaned and
    boned (see pages 80–1)
lemon wedges and parsley to serve

method

1 Heat the oil and pan fry the onions and garlic over a low heat until softened – approximately 5 minutes. Remove the garlic clove. Preheat the oven to 180°C (350°F/gas 4).

2 Remove the pan from the heat and stir in the breadcrumbs, mustard, chopped parsley, egg yolk and ricotta cheese. Stir in the juice of 2 lemons and season to taste.

3   Using a teaspoon, fill the sardines with the stuffing. Lay a large piece of aluminium foil in an ovenproof dish and place the sardines on top. Add the remaining lemon juice and zest, fold the edges of the foil over and pinch to seal. Bake for 30 minutes.

Rolled and filled herrings

I don't understand why people don't eat more of this great oily fish as it is so good for you, very inexpensive and, like mackerel and sardines, very versatile in the way you cook it.

SERVES: 4

Preparation time: 20 minutes
Cooking time: 30 minutes

4 whole fresh medium herrings,
   scaled and heads removed
1 tablespoon extra virgin olive oil
1 garlic clove, crushed
75g fresh breadcrumbs
15g sundried tomatoes, chopped
40g smoked mozzarella
1 tablespoon finely chopped
   rosemary
2 tablespoons freshly chopped
   parsley

1 egg yolk
juice of 3 lemons
8 new potatoes, par boiled and cut
   into 1cm slices
2 bunches of cherry tomatoes on
   the vine
175cl white wine
80g sundried tomatoes
sea salt and ground black pepper
1 tablespoon olive oil

Alternative fish:
sardines

method

1 Clean and fillet the herrings

2 Place the garlic, sundried tomatoes, mozzarella, rosemary, parsley, egg yolk and half the lemon juice in a food processor, blend for 1 minute. Add the olive oil and breadcrumbs and blend for a further minute to make a paste.

3 Using a teaspoon spread the paste over one of the fillets and roll to make a 'rollmop'. Place the potatoes at the bottom of a roasting dish, place the herrings on top and then add the cherry tomatoes, sundried tomatoes and white wine. Cook for 30 minutes. Serve 2 fillets per person.

Trout with apples, cider and cream

Not being a great drinker of cider – alcoholic apple juice really – I thought I would try this one day with a bottle of cider someone had given me. It worked brilliantly!

SERVES: 4

Preparation time: 10 minutes plus
   1 hour marinating time
Cooking time: 15 minutes

5 tablespoons olive oil
150ml (5fl oz) lemon juice
3 garlic cloves, crushed
2 tablespoons chopped parsley
3 tablespoons finely chopped chives
4 trout fillets (200g/7oz each)
5 tablespoons cider
40g (1½oz) butter
2 tablespoons cream
1 cooking apple, cut into
   thin slices

method

1 Mix together the oil, lemon juice, garlic, parsley and chives. Place the fillets in this marinade and leave in the fridge for at least 1 hour. Preheat the oven to 160°C (325°F/gas 3).

2 Meanwhile simmer the cider until reduced by half. Reduce the heat and add the butter and cream, stirring to combine until the butter has melted.

3 Pan fry the trout for 3 minutes on each side. Transfer the fish to a serving dish and bake in the preheated oven for 10 minutes.

4 Add the apple slices to the frying pan, sprinkle with some brown sugar and cook over a high heat for about 10 minutes until they are golden brown. Remove apples and add sauce to pan.

5 Serve the trout with the sauce poured over and apple slices laid on top of the fish.

Alternative fish:
salmon, parrot fish, pomfret

Roast mixed fish

For this dish you can pretty much please yourself as to the fish you use but the rule is that it must not smell of fish and it has to be a good quality firm fish. This recipe is great in that you could prepare everything beforehand and put it in the oven at the last minute or as you serve your starters. Very important to finish with a really good extra virgin olive oil.

SERVES: 4

Preparation time: 25 minutes
Cooking time: 25-30 minutes

Herb breadcrumbs

170g (6oz) fresh breadcrumbs
   made from foccacia or ciabatta
   bread
15g (½oz) pine nuts
1 fat garlic clove, crushed
8 fresh basil leaves, torn
30ml (2 tablespoons) chopped,
   fresh flat-leaf parsley
salt and freshly ground black pepper

Seafood

125g (4½oz) tuna fillet
125g (4½oz) salmon fillet
4 raw king prawns
125g (4½oz) monkfish fillet
125g (4½oz) swordfish fillet
125g (4½oz) red snapper fillet
45ml (3 tablespoons) extra virgin
   olive oil
lemon wedges, to serve

method

1 Pre-heat the oven to 200°C/400°F/Gas Mark 6.

2 Mix all the ingredients for the breadcrumbs in a food processor for about 1 minute, then season to taste. Place in a shallow plate.

3 Prepare the fish – ensuring that they are free from bones – and split each piece except the king prawns into 4 pieces. Drizzle 15ml (1 tablespoon) of the oil over a baking tray large enough to hold all the fish when laid out flat. Lay the fish out and drizzle a little more oil over the seafood and pat the breadcrumbs onto each piece.

4 Roast the fish for 25–30 minutes until just tender, golden and crisp. Transfer the fish to a large platter and drizzle with the remaining oil. Serve with the lemon wedges and sautéed spinach.

Mixed seafood brochettes

This is another recipe where you can choose which ever fish you like but remember it is a skewer so the fish needs to be firm and of good quality. Make this recipe in advance and cook in the oven or in the summer on a BBQ. To make the brochettes, use eight 25cm (10in) bamboo skewers but soak them first in cold water to prevent the food from sticking.

SERVES: 4

Preparation time: 35 minutes
Cooking time: 20 minutes

Coconut rice
400g (14oz) long-grain rice, washed and drained
200ml (7fl oz) canned coconut milk
15ml (1 tablespoon) granulated sugar

Herb sauce
300ml (2 tablespoons) sesame seed oil
2 garlic cloves, crushed
1 fresh green chilli, seeded and finely chopped
1 stick of lemon grass, finely chopped
200ml (7fl oz) canned coconut milk
15ml (1 teaspoon) palm sugar or brown sugar
juice of 1 lime
8 fresh kaffir lime leaves, shredded
300ml (10fl oz) double cream
45g (1½oz) finely chopped fresh coriander leaves
salt and freshly ground pepper

Brochettes
8 red cherry tomatoes
1 medium courgette, trimmed and cut into 8 thin slices
½ medium aubergine, cut lengthways, then into 8 x 2.5cm (1in) pieces
125g (4½oz) tuna fillet
125g (4½oz) salmon fillet
125g (4½oz) monkfish fillet
125g (4½oz) swordfish fillet
125g (4½oz) red snapper fillet
8 fresh kaffir lime leaves
4 raw king prawns
25ml (1½ tablespoons) peanut oil

method

1 Place the rice, coconut milk and granulated sugar in a large pan and cover with enough cold water to bring the liquid about 2.5cm (1in) above the rice. Bring to the boil, reduce heat, cover and simmer for 10 minutes until all the liquid has been absorbed. Remove from the heat and keep the pan covered for 10 minutes to allow the rice to steam until tender.

2 Meanwhile, heat the oil in a saucepan, add the garlic, chilli, lemon grass and stir-fry for 2–3 minutes until soft but not brown. Stir in the coconut milk, sugar, lime juice and lime leaves and cook for 2 minutes. Stir in the cream and cook for 10 minutes to reduce slightly.

3 Wrap each tomato with a courgette piece and thread one on each skewer. Add an aubergine piece to each. Cut all the fish into 4 pieces and randomly thread on the skewers, adding a lime leaf or two in between the fish. End with a prawn. Brush the brochettes with oil and season all over to taste.

4 Pre-heat a ridged cast-iron grill pan and brush with a little oil.

5 Place the brochettes on the grill pan and cook, turning several times, for 6–7 minutes until the fish are tender and the prawns turn pink.

6 Meanwhile, add the coriander leaves to the sauce, season to taste and heat through for 1–2 minutes.

7 Divide the rice among 4 large serving plates, place 2 brochettes on top, then spoon the sauce over them. Serve immediately.

1 This method for cleaning and boning sardines can also be used for anchovies and small herrings or mackerel.

2 Holding the fish by the tail, run the back of a knife down the sides of the fish to remove any scales.

3 Remove all the fins from the sardine using a pair of scissors.

4 Using a pair of scissors, make an incision in the belly near the tail and cut towards the head.

Sardines with spaghetti Sicilian style

Sardines, like mackerel, are very good for you. Both are also very versatile and can be cooked in a variety of ways. As I'm Italian, this method is obviously one of my favourites.

SERVES: 4

Preparation time: 15 minutes
Cooking time: 15 minutes

12 fresh sardines, cleaned and boned
250ml (9fl oz) olive oil
1 onion, chopped
25g (1oz) fresh dill, chopped
55g (2oz) toasted pine nuts
25g (1oz) raisins, soaked
salt and freshly ground black pepper
450g (1lb) spaghetti
75g (2½oz) flour

method

1 Rinse the sardines under water and pat them dry. Open them out flat and cut in half lengthways.

2 Heat 2 tablespoons of the oil in a heavy pan, add the onion and cook over a medium heat for 5–8 minutes, stirring occasionally, until golden. Lower the heat, add the dill and continue cooking for a further 2 minutes. Stir in the pine nuts and raisins, season to taste with salt and pepper and set aside (keeping it warm).

3 Bring a pan of salted water to the boil and add the spaghetti. Cook for the time stated on the packet instructions. It should be *al dente* – slightly firm to the bite.

4 Meanwhile, heat the remaining oil in a pan. Dust the sardines with flour, shaking off any excess. Add the sardines to the oil and fry for 2–3 minutes. Drain on paper towels.

5 Drain the spaghetti and return it to the pan. Add the onion mixture and toss well. Transfer the spaghetti to a large serving plate and arrange the sardines on top. Serve immediately.

Alternative fish:
anchovies, small herrings

5 Pull out the fish's innards and discard.

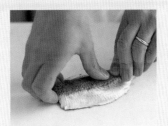

6 Cut off the head of the sardine and discard. Wash the sardine thoroughly under cold water.

7 Place the sardine on a flat board, skin side up, and push the backbone down with your fingers until the fish is almost flat against the board.

8 Turn the sardine over and pull out the backbone.

Fried whitebait with paprika

Some people are very funny about this classic whitebait dish as you eat the whole fish, bones and all. I've seen some customers trying to fillet whitebait, but this is a waste of time. Not only will you end up with hardly any meat, but the best flavour is in the bones.

SERVES: 4

Preparation time: 5 minutes plus
   1 hour marinating time
Cooking time: 3 minutes

500g (1lb 2oz) whitebait
2 teaspoons sea salt
2 tablespoons plain flour
1 tablespoon paprika
2 teaspoons finely chopped parsley
salt and freshly ground black pepper
vegetable oil for frying
lemon wedges, tartare sauce and
   chopped parsley to serve
   (optional)

method

1 Combine the whitebait and sea salt in a dish, mix well and refrigerate for 1 hour.

2 Sift the flour and paprika into a bowl, add the parsley and season with salt and pepper.

3 Heat the vegetable oil in either a deep-fat fryer or a large saucepan. When it is hot enough, a pinch of flour dropped into it will sizzle immediately.

4 Toss some of the whitebait in the flour and paprika, then shake off excess flour and deep fry in 2 batches for 2–3 minutes each batch until a pale gold colour. Drain onto paper towels.

5 Serve immediately, with lemon wedges and tartare sauce and sprinkled with more chopped parsley if desired.

Alternative fish:
sprats, anchovies

Boneless herring dipped in egg and fried in garlic butter

I love eggy fried fish as it always gives a lovely golden colour to the dish. If you are pan frying any fish in breadcrumbs or another coating, make sure you flour the fish first. This will ensure the coatings stick to the fish.

SERVES: 4

Preparation time: 10 minutes
Cooking time: 8 minutes

plain flour for coating
salt and freshly ground black pepper
75g (2½oz) unsalted butter
2 tablespoons finely chopped garlic
2 eggs, whisked
8 herring fillets

method

1 Season the flour with the salt and pepper and place in a shallow dish. In a large frying pan, heat the butter. Add the garlic and cook over a medium heat for 2 minutes. Make sure you do not burn the garlic as this will ruin the flavour.

2 Place the beaten eggs into a shallow dish. Dip the herrings in the flour, then into the egg. Fry the coated fish in the garlic butter for 8 minutes, turning occasionally.

3 Serve on a plate with the remaining garlic butter poured over.

Alternative fish:
sardines, mackerel

Right: Fried whitebait with paprika

Spring onion pancakes with gravadlax

Salmon is such a versatile fish and gravadlax makes an expensive but impressive dish to prepare for friends. You can, of course, buy ready-made gravadlax, but I think making it yourself is what makes this dish special. If you are using smoked salmon or haddock, just lay the slices on top of the pancake.

SERVES: 4

Preparation time: 20 minutes plus
   pancake mix to rest overnight
Cooking time: 8 minutes

2 eggs
225ml (8fl oz) milk
175g (6oz) butter
125g (4½oz) plain flour
2½ teaspoons baking powder
½ teaspoon salt
55g (2oz) spring onions, chopped
juice of 2 lemons
salt and freshly ground black pepper
1 cucumber
125g (4½oz) baby spinach
16 slices gravadlax

method

1 Melt 40g (1½oz) of the butter and allow to cool. Place in a bowl with the eggs and milk and whisk until combined. Sift the flour, baking powder and salt into a bowl, make a well in the centre and gradually add the egg mix, beating until the batter is smooth. Leave in the fridge overnight.

2 Heat a nonstick frying pan and ladle 4 tablespoons of batter into the pan. You should be able to make 2 pancakes at the same time. Sprinkle each pancake with 1 tablespoon of chopped spring onions and cook for about 2 minutes, or until bubbles begin to appear on the surface. Turn pancakes over and cook the other side. Keep the pancakes warm while cooking remaining ones.

3 Make lemon butter by heating the lemon juice and whisking in the remaining butter, a bit at a time, until melted. Season with salt and pepper. Cut cucumber into ribbons with a potato peeler.

4 Place a pancake on each plate and top with baby spinach, 4 slices of gravadlax and a pile of cucumber ribbons. Spoon lemon butter around the pancake and serve.

Alternative fish:
smoked salmon, haddock

Marinated anchovies

I hold monthly masterclasses in my restaurants and this is one of the dishes I teach: it is the most requested recipe of the course. If the anchovies are covered in oil, you can keep them in the fridge for up to 3 weeks.

SERVES: 2

Preparation time: 10 minutes plus
   15 hours (total) marinating time

1 bottle white wine vinegar
1 glass white wine
juice of 3 lemons
5 tablespoons sea salt
4 bay leaves
2 sprigs thyme
8 garlic cloves
12 fresh anchovies, boned
2 chillies, finely chopped
2 tablespoons chopped parsley
5 tablespoons extra virgin olive oil

method

1 In a bowl, mix together white wine vinegar, white wine, lemon juice, sea salt, bay leaves, thyme and 5 whole garlic cloves. Place the anchovies in a flat dish and pour over this marinade. Leave to marinate in a cool place for at least 12 hours.

2 Remove anchovies from the marinade and dip into a bowl of water. Pat dry with paper towels and place on a shallow plate.

3 Finely chop remaining garlic cloves and sprinkle over the anchovies with the chopped chilli and parsley. Pour olive oil over, making sure all the fish are covered. Marinate for at least 3 hours before serving.

Alternative fish:
baby sardines, sprats

*Right: Spring onion pancake
with gravadlax*

MAKING GRAVADLAX

1 Place the salmon skin side down on a plate and pat crushed sea salt and crushed black peppercorns onto the top. Pour brandy over.

2 Cover the top with chopped dill. Cover with cling film and place a weighted object on top of the fish. Place in the fridge overnight.

3 Remove from the fridge and carefully lift out the salmon. Using a sharp knife, gently remove the skin from the salmon.

4 Using a very sharp knife, slice the salmon lengthways as thinly as you like.

Seared tuna with sticky rice, wasabi and soy sauce

This very lightly cooked recipe is fantastic! I don't understand people eating well-done tuna – you might as well eat tinned tuna. If, like me, you need to watch your weight, leave out the rice and serve with rocket and Parmesan salad.

SERVES: 4

Preparation time: 10 minutes
Cooking time: 3 minutes

4 tablespoons olive oil
½ teaspoon salt
3 tablespoons freshly cracked black
   pepper
2 teaspoons paprika
small fillet of tuna (600g/1lb 5oz)
300g (10½oz) sticky rice, cooked
soy sauce and wasabi to serve

Alternative fish:
salmon, swordfish,
sea bass

method

1 Heat a frying pan and add the oil. In a bowl mix together the salt, pepper and paprika and use to season the tuna fillet. Place the tuna in the pan of hot oil and sear for 1 minute on each side. Remove from the pan and leave to cool.

2 Divide the sticky rice between 4 teacups, pat down, then turn out onto 4 plates. Slice the tuna very thinly and place over the rice. Serve with the soy sauce and wasabi.

Salmon carpaccio with pine nuts and soy sauce

Carpaccio, which translates as 'raw', is normally associated with beef but adapting it for fish is great too. As with sushi and sashimi, you must make sure that you use only fish that is extremely fresh, so find a good fishmonger or large market.

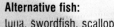

1 Holding the blade of a very sharp knife nearly horizontal to the side of salmon, slice it very thinly. You should be able to see the blade through the fish.

SERVES: 4

Preparation time: 40 minutes

500g (1lb 2oz) sushi-grade salmon
1 tablespoon extra virgin olive oil
1 tablespoon lime juice
2 tablespoons soy sauce
salt and freshly ground black pepper
1 fennel bulb, thinly sliced
3 tablespoons pine nuts, toasted
   and crushed
½ medium cucumber, thinly sliced
2 tablespoons finely chopped
   spring onions
grated zest of 1 lime

method

1 Wrap the salmon in cling film and freeze for 20–30 minutes until the fish is partly frozen; this will make it easier to slice.

2 Remove the salmon and unwrap. Using a sharp knife or a slicer cut into thin slices across the grain.

3 To make the dressing, whisk together the olive oil, lime juice and soy sauce and season to taste.

4 Place the fennel in the centre of each serving plate and arrange salmon slices around the outside. Scatter crushed pine nuts, cucumber, spring onions and lime zest over the salmon and then drizzle with some of the dressing. Leave in the fridge for 1 hour before serving with small bowls of remaining dressing.

Alternative fish:
tuna, swordfish, scallops

Spicy mackerel pâté

Fish pâté used to be extremely popular and I think it is time we brought it back into favour. Try this recipe and see if you agree. It also makes a great snack for your kids when they get home from school and will stop them from filling up with crisps.

SERVES: 4

Preparation time: 15 minutes plus 4 hours chilling time

4 smoked, peppered mackerel fillets (150g/5½oz each), skinned and flaked
225g (8oz) ricotta cheese
2 garlic cloves, finely chopped
juice of 1 lemon
2 tablespoons chopped chives
1 tablespoon Worcestershire sauce
salt and cayenne pepper to taste
chopped chives and toasted brown bread to serve

method

1 Place the smoked mackerel, ricotta cheese, garlic, lemon juice and chives in a food processor and blend until the mixture is fairly smooth, then add the Worcestershire sauce and salt and cayenne pepper to taste. Blend for a further 1 minute to ensure it is well mixed.

2 Spoon the pâté into a buttered dish, cover with cling film and chill in the fridge for 4 hours.

3 Garnish with some more chives and serve with toasted brown bread.

Alternative fish:
haddock, sardines

Smoked eel, endive and radicchio salad

I think that you either love eel or hate it – there's no in-between with this fish. I like to make this salad when it is a beautiful summer's day – it's lovely and crisp.

SERVES: 4

Preparation time: 15 minutes

450g (1lb) smoked eel fillets, skinned
2 endive heads
4 radicchio leaves
2 tablespoons sultanas
4 spring onions, sliced

Dressing
juice of 1 orange and zest of ½
juice of 1 lime and zest of ½
1 teaspoon sugar
1 teaspoon wholegrain mustard
6 tablespoons olive oil
2 tablespoons chopped parsley
salt and freshly ground black pepper

method

1 Cut the eel into strips about 4cm (1½in) wide.

2 To make the dressing, place the orange juice in a pan and add the orange and lime zests and the sugar. Bring to the boil, then lower the heat and reduce by half. Leave to cool completely.

3 Whisk together the lime juice, mustard and olive oil, then add the reduced orange juice. Stir in the parsley and season to taste.

4 Arrange the endive and radicchio leaves on 4 plates and top with eel strips. Scatter over sultanas and spring onions, then drizzle over dressing.

Alternative fish:
smoked trout

Right: Smoked eel, endive and radicchio salad

Baby smoked herring with beetroot and sour cream

My fish supplier delivered me smoked herring by mistake one day so I concocted this great salad. It is now a firm favourite and has become a regular fixture on the Salad Bar at Zilli Café.

SERVES: 4

Preparation time: 10 minutes

250g (9oz) smoked baby herrings, cut into slices
1 small cooking apple, cored, peeled and diced
6 gherkins, diced
1 teaspoon refined sugar
1 teaspoon white wine vinegar
150ml (5fl oz) sour cream
1 cooked beetroot, diced
1 lollo rosso lettuce
1 lollo biondo lettuce
½ red onion, sliced

method

1 Place the herrings, apple, gherkins, sugar and vinegar into a bowl and mix well together. Add the sour cream and combine, then gently fold in the diced beetroot. Place in the fridge to chill.

2 Serve on the lollo rosso and lollo biondo lettuce and garnish with the red onion slices.

Alternative fish:
smoked sardines

Smoked trout and potato salad

Trout, hot- or cold-smoked or fresh or otherwise, is a great fish. My favourite is salmon or sea trout as I find river trout too strong. This simple recipe came to me years ago for salmon but it is just as delicious made with trout.

SERVES: 4

Preparation time: 20 minutes
Cooking time: 10–15 minutes

100ml (3½fl oz) extra virgin olive oil
3 tablespoons lemon juice
1 tablespoon red wine vinegar
1 garlic clove crushed with sea salt
freshly ground black pepper
2 tablespoons chopped mint
2 tablespoons chopped parsley
2 tablespoons finely chopped
   spring onions
1 red pepper, seeded and thinly
   sliced
1 stick celery, sliced
1 tablespoon capers
500g (1lb 2oz) unpeeled waxy
   potatoes
250g (9oz) cold-smoked rainbow
   trout, skin and bones removed

Lemon mayonnaise
1 egg yolk
zest of 1 lemon
3 tablespoons lemon juice
sea salt and freshly ground black
   pepper
100ml (3½fl oz) mild oil

Alternative fish:
smoked mackerel

method

1 To make the mayonnaise, place the egg yolk, lemon zest and juice and salt and pepper to taste in a bowl or food processor and whisk until combined. Add the oil drop by drop, whisking constantly. When it starts to thicken, add the oil in a steady stream until fully combined. If mayonnaise is too thick, add a tablespoon of warm water. Store in the fridge.

2 Place the olive oil, lemon juice, vinegar, garlic, salt and pepper in a bowl and whisk. Stir in mint, parsley, spring onions, pepper, celery and capers.

3 Cook the potatoes in salted water until tender. Drain and allow to cool for a few minutes, or until you can handle them, before peeling and slicing them.

4 Add the potatoes to the dressing while they are still warm and stir gently to combine.

5 Divide the potato salad between 4 plates and top each with some smoked trout. Drizzle with lemon mayonnaise to serve.

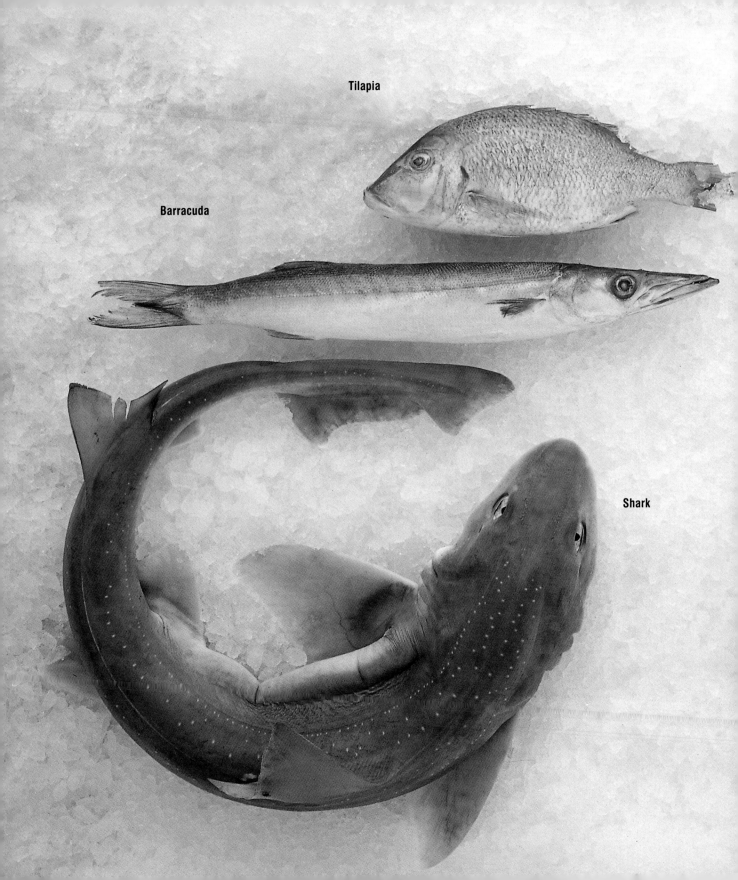

Tilapia

Barracuda

Shark

Pomfret

Exotic Fish

Red emperor

Parrot fish

Barramundi

Yellowtail snapper

Exotic Fish

When I first came to the UK, the likelihood of finding any of these fish was very rare. Now, thanks to improved storing of fish and importing, many more exotic fish varieties can be found at good fishmongers or in good markets or supermarkets. This is a huge section of fish and it would be impossible for me to name them all, so I have tried to choose those that are fairly easily available all over the world. (Don't be confused by my list of exotic fish: people living in other countries – Australia, for example – will think of barramundi and barracuda as common fare and will probably consider some of the fish I have included in other chapters more exotic.) Most exotic fish that you can buy in the UK will be frozen. When the fish are caught, they are immediately put in the freezer on the boats before being exported and the quality of these 'frozen as fresh' fish is surprisingly good. Don't be put off by the fact that you are not acquainted with these fish: while they might look different to the fish that you are used to, they are nonetheless very tasty and can often be prepared, cooked and eaten in much the same way as any more well-known fish.

BARRACUDA genus *Sphyraena*
Barracudas are usually found in warm, tropical regions. They are swift and powerful, small scaled and slender in form, with two well-separated dorsal fins, a jutting lower jaw and a large mouth with many sharp, large teeth. Size varies from rather small to as large as 1.2–1.8m (4–6 feet) in the great barracuda of the Atlantic, Caribbean and the Pacific. They are good, fighting sporting fishes, and the smaller ones make good eating. Barracudas are bold, inquisitive and fearsome fish, which may be dangerous to humans. (The great barracuda is known to have been involved in attacks on swimmers.) Barracuda is quite an oily fish, so avoid cooking it with butter or cream.

BARRAMUNDI *Lates calcarifer*
This fish has gained a reputation of being one of Australia's finest eating fish. Barramundi are excellent table fish with relatively few bones and a firm, white, fine-grained flesh with a delicate flavour that can be prepared in a number of ways. They resemble giant perch and can grow to a large size, sometimes weighing more than 20kg (44lb), though fish of 5–6kg (11–13lb) are more usual.

DORADE *Coryphaenidae hippurus*
Also known as dolphin fish and mahi mahi, the dorade tapers sharply from head to tail and is a bright, greeny blue fish with yellow down its sides. When stressed, it flashes neon purple. Dorade has a wonderfully tender white flesh and when cooked has a rich succulent flavour, which lends itself to any recipe.

MARLIN genus *Makaira*
There are two main types of marlin – blue and white – and both are a popular catch with sports fishermen. Marlin is normally sold in steaks and is similar to swordfish and tuna with flesh that is a slightly darker white colour than that of swordfish. Although it makes good eating, marlin does not have the same delicate flavour as swordfish.

PARROT FISH family Scaridae
It always seems a pity to eat this beautiful-looking fish, but when you combine parrot fish with strong flavours they make for great eating. Parrot fish are bony, marine fish whose teeth have fused to form an extremely hard beak, which enables them to bite off pieces of coral. This, with seaweed and molluscs, forms their principal food. All parrot fish are brilliantly coloured and some may grow to as large as 1m (40in) in length, although they are generally smaller than this.

POMFRET *Pampus argenteus*
Pomfret, known as butterfish in the USA, are normally about 20cm (8in) long. The pomfret's back is a leaden bluish colour, its sides are paler and it has a silvery belly. The body is thin and deep with almost no scales and resembles that of a flat fish. Pomfret look like angel fish and although they don't have much flesh, what they do have is lovely with a strong, firm, texture. Pomfret is becoming increasingly popular in the UK and is one of few fish species worldwide deemed to be under-exploited.

RED EMPEROR *Lutjanus sebae*
Red emperors belong to the tropical snapper and sea perch family and are salmon pink to red in colour with pink fins tipped with bright crimson and three distinctive darker red bands. They are normally fished in the Australian tropical seas and can weigh more than 18kg (40lb), although an average fish is usually around 2–7kg (4½–15½lb). Red emperor has delicate white flesh and makes excellent eating.

SHARK genus *Alopias* and others
Shark have a cartilaginous skeleton and lack the sort of small bones that put some people off eating fish. Like skate, they tend to have an ammonia smell, but this disappears with cooking. If however, you are given a cooked piece of shark and it still smells of ammonia, it is old and should be sent back to the kitchen.

TILAPIA genus *Tilapia*
Although they are found mainly in tropical seas, tilapia can live in fresh water or salt water. Most fresh tilapia come from Columbia and Costa Rica, while frozen tilapia is imported from the Far East. Tilapia are now available all year round in the USA where they are farmed. Tilapia have a huge range of colours, from grey to bright red. The meat is white and firm, but is bland, so lends itself to spicy dishes.

YELLOWTAIL SNAPPER *Ocyurus chrysurus*
Yellowtail snappers are easily distinguished by the yellow stripes down the side of their body and the yellow spots on their back. They feed on small fish and normally weigh around 1.4–2.25kg (3–5lb). They are very popular in the Caribbean, where they are found in large numbers.

Pomfret with tamarind and chilli sauce

While this is an unusual fish in both looks and taste, it is perfect for the barbecue. With the additional strong flavours of tamarind and chilli, this is a dish well worth making.

SERVES: 4

Preparation time: 10 minutes
Cooking time: 10 minutes

4 pomfret (250g/9oz each), cleaned
6 spring onions, chopped
3 tablespoons soy sauce
12 cherry tomatoes, halved
2 tablespoons chopped fresh coriander

Sauce
55g (2oz) tamarind pulp
7 tablespoons boiling water
2 shallots, coarsely chopped
1 stalk lemongrass, peeled and chopped
1 fresh red chilli, seeded and chopped
½ teaspoon finely chopped fresh root ginger
1 teaspoon soft brown sugar
3 tablespoons nam pla (fish sauce)

method

1 Slash the pomfret 3 times on each side with a sharp knife and place in a shallow dish.

2 Fill the slashes with spring onions and pour over the soy sauce. Turn the fish to coat both sides in the soy sauce. Set aside.

3 To make the sauce, put the tamarind in a bowl and add the boiling water. Mash until soft, then tip into a blender and process. Stir in the shallots, lemongrass, chilli, ginger, sugar and fish sauce.

4 Cook the fish on the barbecue with some cherry tomatoes for about 5 minutes on each side, until the skin is crispy and the fish is cooked. Alternatively, heat some oil in a frying pan and cook the fish for about 3 minutes on each side. Spoon over sauce, sprinkle with coriander and serve.

Alternative fish:
bream, mullet

CLEANING AND SCALING SNAPPER

1 Holding on to the tail, drag a sharp knife along the fish to remove scales. If you are nervous about cutting the fish, use the back of the knife.

2 Using a sharp pair of scissors, cut off all the fins, then cut open the belly of the fish from the tail to the head.

3 Using your fingers, reach inside the cavity of the fish and pull out and discard all the guts. Rinse the fish under cold water.

Spicy baked yellowtail snapper with pine nuts

If you can't find a whole fish then use fillets, but roast the fillet for only half the time stated for a whole fish. Pine nuts work particularly well with fish, but if you are unfortunate enough to be allergic to nuts, you can omit them.

SERVES: 4

Preparation time: 10 minutes plus 2 hours marinating time
Cooking time: 35 minutes

375g (13oz) yellowtail snapper, cleaned and scaled
½ teaspoon salt
juice of 2 lemons
4 tablespoons extra virgin olive oil
2 onions, sliced
4 garlic cloves, chopped
1 green pepper, seeded and diced
2 fresh green chillies, seeded and finely chopped
½ teaspoon ground turmeric
½ teaspoon curry powder
½ teaspoon ground cumin
115ml (4fl oz) passata
5 fresh tomatoes, peeled and chopped
4 tablespoons chopped fresh coriander
75g (2½oz) pine nuts, toasted

method

1 Using a fork, prick the fish all over then rub with salt. Place on a roasting tray and sprinkle lemon juice all over. Leave to marinate for 2 hours.

2 Preheat the oven to 180°C (350°F/gas 4). Heat the oil in a pan and add the onions and half the garlic and cook until softened. Add the pepper, chillies, turmeric, curry powder and cumin to the pan and cook gently for 2–3 minutes. Stir in the passata, tomatoes and chopped coriander.

3 Sprinkle half the pine nuts over the base of an ovenproof dish and top with half the sauce. Add the fish and its marinade, sprinkle remaining garlic over and then top with the remaining sauce and pine nuts. Cover with aluminium foil and bake in the oven for 30 minutes.

Alternative fish:
red snapper, red bream

Parrot fish with red curry paste

Curry tends to marry well with shellfish but when I tried it with this kind of fish it was equally successful. Green curry paste will not work, however, as the flavour of the curry, rather than adding to the fish, will overwhelm it.

SERVES: 6

Preparation time: 10 minutes
Cooking time: 30 minutes

1 small grapefruit
1 blood orange
1 lemon
1 parrot fish (1.4kg/3lb), cleaned
   and scaled
salt and freshly ground black pepper
2 tablespoons Thai red curry paste
5 shallots, halved
3 tablespoons olive oil
4 tablespoons white wine
40g (1½oz) butter, melted

Alternative fish:
bream, sea bass

method

1 Preheat the oven to 190˚C (375˚F/gas 5). Using a potato peeler, remove the rind from the grapefruit, blood orange and lemon and cut into strips. Peel and discard the white pith from the fruits. Cut the grapefruit and blood orange into segments, reserving the juice, and cut the lemon into thick slices.

2 Season the inside of the fish with salt and pepper and make 3 diagonal slashes in the side of the fish. Fill the inside of the fish with the lemon slices and half of the citrus rinds. Spread the curry paste over the top of the fish making sure to get some in the slashes.

3 Lay the fish in a roasting pan, add the shallot halves and drizzle over 1½ tablespoons of oil. Roast in the oven for about 15 minutes. Remove from the oven, carefully turn the fish and stir the shallots, drizzle with remaining oil and roast for a further 10–15 minutes until cooked through.

4 Remove the fish from the pan and keep warm. Skim off excess oil and add the wine and fruit juices to the pan. Bring to the boil and stir in remaining rinds. Whisk in the butter and spoon the sauce and shallots around the fish. Serve with the grapefruit and orange segments and lemon slices.

PAN FRYING WHOLE FISH

1 Insert into the cavity of the fish any herbs or other stuffing ingredients that you wish to use. Sprinkle the fish with sea salt.

2 Place the fish on a plate of seasoned flour and pat flour all over the fish, making sure that you cover it completely.

3 Wrap the tail in foil to prevent it burning. Place the fish in a pan of hot oil and pan fry over medium heat for 10 minutes on each side.

4 If you wish, add some sauce to the pan just before the fish is cooked. This will ensure that the fish absorbs the sauce flavours.

Tilapia with fruit sauce

I love cooking with fruit, especially mango or papaya, and tilapia cooked whole like this is fantastic. Tilapia comes from the Caribbean but is now being farmed in the USA and is becoming more readily available in the UK too.

SERVES: 4

Preparation time: 15 minutes plus
  overnight marinating time
Cooking time: 40 minutes

4 tilapia (350g/12oz each), cleaned
juice of ½ lemon
2 garlic cloves, crushed
½ teaspoon dried thyme
2 tablespoons chopped spring
  onions
vegetable oil for frying
flour for coating
2 tablespoons peanut oil
1 tablespoon butter
1 onion, finely chopped
3 tomatoes, peeled and finely
  chopped
1 teaspoon ground turmeric
4 tablespoons white wine
1 fresh green chilli, seeded and
  finely chopped
600ml (20fl oz) fish stock
1 teaspoon sugar
1 medium under-ripe mango
1 tablespoon chopped fresh parsley

method

1 Place the fish in a bowl and pour the lemon juice over, then rub in the garlic, thyme and some salt and freshly ground black pepper. Place some of the spring onions in each fish and then cover the bowl with cling film and leave overnight.

2 Heat some vegetable oil in a large heavy-based frying pan. Coat the fish with flour, making sure you shake off any excess. Fry the fish on both sides over a medium heat for a few minutes until golden brown. Remove from pan and set to one side.

3 Heat the peanut oil and butter in another pan, add the onion and cook over a low heat for 4–5 minutes until softened. Stir in the tomatoes, turn up the heat and cook for a few more minutes.

4 Add the turmeric, white wine, chilli, fish stock and sugar to the pan and stir well. Bring to the boil, then lower the heat, cover and simmer for 12 minutes.

5 Add the fish to the pan and cook for a further 15 minutes until the fish is cooked through. Peel, stone and chop the mango, stir it into the sauce and cook for a further 2 minutes.

6 Serve the fish on a platter with the fruit sauce poured over. Garnish with the chopped parsley and serve immediately, with some minted new potatoes if desired.

Alternative fish:
John Dory, grey mullet, sea bream

Dorade poached in milk with herb sauce

Milk poaching is a great way of cooking that I first used for salmon – it was lovely and moist. Dorade also tastes wonderful roasted with garlic and rosemary.

Alternative fish:
salmon, cod

SERVES: 4

Preparation time: 10 minutes
Cooking time: 20 minutes

4 dorade fillets (190g/6½oz each)
2 tablespoons lemon juice
½ teaspoon salt
½ teaspoon ground black pepper
750ml (26fl oz) milk
125ml (4½fl oz) fish stock
1 white onion, chopped
2 teaspoons chopped fresh thyme
1 tablespoon black peppercorns
1 tablespoon chopped fresh parsley
roasted leeks to serve (optional)

method

1 Place the fish in a shallow dish and rub with the lemon juice and sprinkle with the salt and pepper, set aside to marinate.

2 In a saucepan combine the milk, fish stock, onion, thyme and peppercorns and bring to the boil. Gently slide in the fish fillets and simmer for 15 minutes. Remove the fish and keep warm.

3 Bring the milk back to the boil and reduce the liquid by three quarters, then add the parsley. Serve the fish covered in the herb sauce, with roasted leeks if desired.

Marlin with black pepper and cream sauce

This is traditionally a sauce that is used with steak, but I tried it one day with fish and really loved it. Use a firm fish as delicate fish will be swamped by the rich sauce.

Alternative fish:
tuna, swordfish

SERVES: 4

Preparation time: 10 minutes plus
  1 hour marinating time
Cooking time: 35 minutes

4 marlin steaks (175g/6oz each)
1 teaspoon sea salt
2 tablespoons olive oil
1 tablespoon lemon juice
400g (14oz) potatoes, peeled and
  quartered
25g (1oz) butter
1 tablespoon olive oil
pinch saffron strands, melted in
  hot water

Black pepper sauce
olive oil for stir frying
1 tablespoon chopped onion
2 tablespoons chopped garlic
1 tablespoon sugar
4 tablespoons cream
2 tablespoons oyster sauce
1 tablespoon soy sauce
2 tablespoons cracked
  black pepper

method

1 Marinate the marlin in the sea salt, oil and lemon juice.

2 To make the sauce, stir fry the onion until it becomes translucent. Stir in the garlic, sugar, cream, oyster sauce, soy sauce and black pepper. Simmer for 15 minutes over a low heat.

3 Meanwhile, cook the potatoes until soft, remove from the heat and strain. Add the butter and olive oil and mash. When smooth, add the saffron and, using a spatula, mix until completely incorporated. Keep warm.

4 Pan fry the marlin in some of the marinade for 7 minutes on each side. Serve with saffron mash and black pepper sauce.

Shark steaks Moroccan style

I created this recipe in the '80s when shark was very cheap, but I still put it on the menu every now and then and it is very popular. It holds special memories for me – I cooked it for my wife Nikki the first time I met her in my restaurant.

SERVES: 4

Preparation time: 15 minutes plus
    2 hours marinating time
Cooking time: 10 minutes

150ml (5fl oz) olive oil
1 tablespoon paprika
2 teaspoons harissa (chilli sauce)
2 teaspoons cumin
2 garlic cloves, crushed
juice of 2 lemons
salt and freshly ground black pepper
3 tablespoons chopped coriander
2 tablespoons chopped mint
4 shark steaks (185g/6½oz each)
lemon wedges to serve

method

1   In a bowl, mix together the olive oil, paprika, harissa, cumin, garlic and lemon juice. Season, then stir in the chopped coriander and mint.

2   Pour the marinade into a non-metallic dish large enough to fit the shark steaks in a single layer. Turn the shark steaks over in the dish to ensure that they are evenly coated with the marinade. Cover the dish with cling film and place in the fridge for 2 hours.

3   Heat the grill to medium-high, then grill the shark steaks for 5 minutes on each side until just cooked, turning the steaks once and basting them several times with the marinade. Serve immediately with lemon wedges.

Alternative fish:
monkfish, swordfish, cod

Braised barramundi with shellfish

Some of you may not be very familiar with this fish. Well neither was I, but I highly recommend it. It is very well known as lungfish in Australia, where you can buy it fresh; in the UK only frozen barramundi is normally available.

SERVES: 4

Preparation time: 10 minutes
Cooking time: 15 minutes

2 tablespoons olive oil
1 onion, thinly sliced
1 yellow pepper, seeded and cut
    into strips
400ml (14fl oz) passata
3 tablespoons dry white wine
2 courgettes, sliced
450g (1lb) mixed shellfish
350g (12oz) skinned barramundi
    fillets, cut into 5cm (2in) chunks
salt and freshly ground black pepper
juice of ½ lemon
2 tablespoons shredded fresh basil
noodles or pasta to serve (optional)

method

1   Heat the oil in a large frying pan, add the onion and pepper and stir fry for 2 minutes until the onion is translucent.

2   Stir the passata and the white wine into the pan and bring to the boil. Lower the heat and simmer for 2 minutes.

3   Add the courgettes, mixed shellfish and barramundi, cover and cook over a low heat for about 5 minutes, stirring occasionally. Season to taste with salt, pepper and lemon juice, and simmer for a further 4 minutes, then stir in half the shredded basil.

4   Garnish with remaining basil and serve with noodles or pasta, if desired.

Alternative fish:
cod, salmon, halibut, swordfish, snapper, ocean perch

Left: Shark steaks Moroccan style

Barbecued red emperor with herb relish

This fish is extremely popular in Australia where it is also called the emperor snapper fish. Barbecuing has to be one of the best methods of cooking red emperor or indeed any kind of fish – it's lovely and fresh as well as healthy.

SERVES: 4

Preparation time: 10 minutes plus
   2 hours marinating time
Cooking time: 10 minutes

4 tablespoons olive oil
2 tablespoons chopped fresh dill
1 tablespoon chopped fresh parsley
1 tablespoon chopped fresh lemon
   thyme
1 tablespoon fresh lemon juice
1 teaspoon minced garlic
2 tablespoons finely chopped red
   onion
2 tablespoons sherry vinegar
4 red emperor fillets (200g/7oz
   each)
salt and freshly ground black pepper

method

1 Mix together 2 tablespoons of olive oil, dill, parsley, lemon thyme, lemon juice, garlic, red onion and sherry vinegar. Set aside for the flavours to combine.

2 Rub the fish fillets with the remaining olive oil and season both sides. Place the fillets on a hot barbecue or grill and cook for 5 minutes on each side.

3 Remove fish from the grill and serve topped with the herb relish.

Alternative fish:
snapper, mullet

Barracuda shiitake teriyaki

This is a very well-known fish that is normally cooked on the barbecue because of its lovely firm flesh. However, as I love teriyaki, I thought I would try cooking it this way, and this recipe is a definite winner.

SERVES: 4

Preparation time: 10 minutes plus
   40 minutes marinating time
Cooking time: 15 minutes

4 barracuda steaks (175g/6oz each)
salt and freshly ground black pepper
175g (6oz) shiitake mushrooms,
   sliced
150ml (5fl oz) teriyaki sauce
225g (8oz) white radish, peeled
2 large carrots, peeled

method

1 Season the steaks, place in a dish in a single layer and set aside for 20 minutes. Scatter over the sliced mushrooms, pour over the teriyaki sauce and set aside to marinate for at least 20 minutes, or as long as possible.

2 Drain the barracuda, reserving the marinade and mushrooms, and cook on a preheated barbecue for 4 minutes each side.

3 Transfer the mushrooms and marinade to a pan and simmer gently for 4 minutes.

4 Slice the radish and carrots thinly and arrange in a heap on each plate. Top with the fish, pour over the mushroom sauce and serve immediately.

Alternative fish:
dorade, monkfish

Right: Barracuda shiitake teriyaki

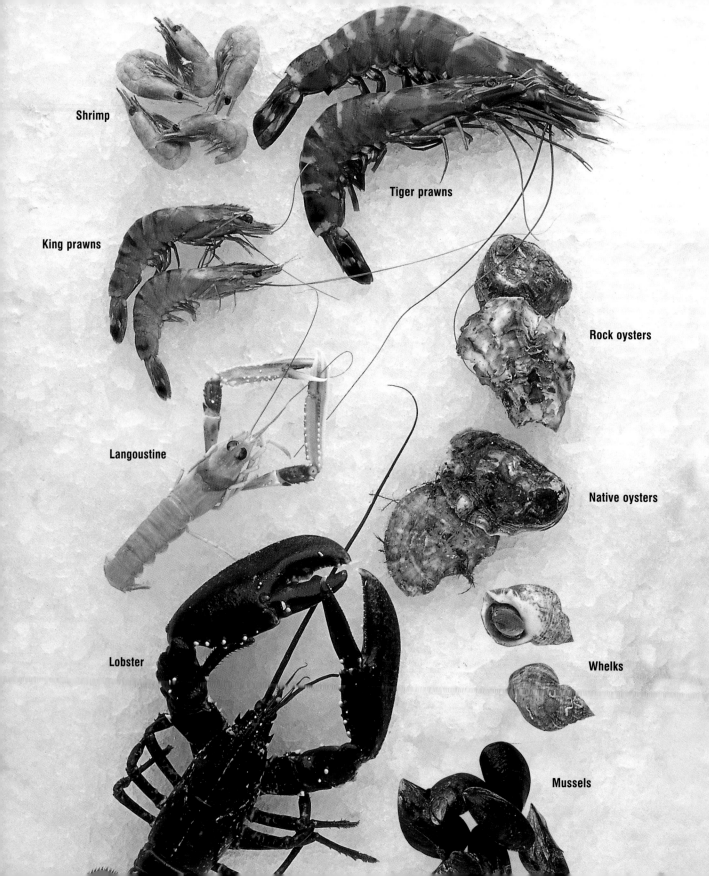

Shrimp

Tiger prawns

King prawns

Rock oysters

Langoustine

Native oysters

Whelks

Lobster

Mussels

Spider crab

Scallops

Shellfish

American (large) clams

Crab

Clams

Razor clams

Shellfish

Aquatic invertebrates are believed to descend from creatures that lived on earth more than 200 million years ago and are divided into two main classes: crustaceans and molluscs. Most crustaceans are marine and include lobsters, crabs and shrimp, but crayfish are found in fresh water. Crustaceans are very odd-looking creatures, but while they may not look like the most attractive of foods, it is well worth the effort involved in removing their delicious flesh. Crustaceans need to be very fresh and are best bought live, but you can also buy them ready cooked, as well, of course, as frozen or canned. Molluscs are divided into bivalves, such as clams, mussels and oysters, which have a hinged shell, and gastropods, which have a single external shell and include abalone, conch, limpets and whelks. There are two important things to remember when you are preparing molluscs: firstly, they should be soaked in water overnight in order to remove the sand (the exception to this is scallops, which can be simply cleaned), and shells that are open before cooking and those that are closed once cooked should be discarded or you could become ill.

Crustaceans

CRABS

Crabs have evolved so that they can walk or run sideways as well as burrow and swim. Their body is covered in a carapace and they also have a reduced abdomen, which is tucked under the body and is used as a pouch for eggs.

The segmented body has several pairs of legs, of which usually five pairs are for walking and two for sensing and smelling. They also have two pincers for fighting, feeding and display. Crabs adapt to the changing environment and are thought to have advanced senses of smell and taste, which help them to mate and forage.

Crabs are quite adventurous and will travel hundreds of miles in a year for feeding and to breeding grounds. Most crabs are caught far from the shore in baited traps.

Like most crustaceans, crabs shed their shell and grow a new one. While the new shell is growing, it is soft and these so-called soft-shell crabs can be eaten whole (see below).

The sweetest meat is found in female crabs, but they are smaller in size than the males and their claws also tend to contain less flesh.

All crabs should be bought alive rather than cooked. The best way to cook crabs is to put them in cold salted water and bring them to the boil. This will ensure that the meat is tender; if you throw them into boiling water, their muscles contract and this can affect the flavour of the meat.

COMMON/DORSET CRAB *Cancer pagurus*
Small specimens may be found on the shore, although the larger ones are usually found in deeper water. They are often found under rock crevices where they can easily defend themselves with their huge claws. They are very aggressive and care needs to be taken when handling them. Their body is a reddish brown colour and can measure well over 20cm (8in) and their large, powerful claws contain plenty of tasty flesh.

The male waits until the female is 'moulting' in order to mate and holds onto the female waiting for the moulting to be complete. The female carries as many as two million eggs for 7–8 months, but only a few of these survive.

These crabs are scavengers but will also feed on molluscs, which they crush with their large claws.

SPIDER CRAB *Maja squinado*
The spider crab is spiny and pear shaped with long slender legs, thus resembling a large pink spider. Harmless to humans and not particularly aggressive, the spider crab's main defence is to camouflage itself: it has hairs on its shell that hold algae and debris in place, thus blending the crab into its environment.

Spider crabs live in deeper water in the winter, normally in depths up to 120m (nearly 400ft), but come closer to the shore in the summer months when temperatures rise. Like other crabs, the females carry the eggs, which take 60–75 days to mature before the larvae hatch. A female crab may hatch as many as 150,000 larvae.

The spider crabs found in the Atlantic measure about 20cm (8in) across, but there is a giant species that originates around Japan that can grow up to 40cm (16in) and has a claw span of 3m (10ft). This is not a crustacean for arachnophobes!

SOFT-SHELL CRAB
These are blue crabs (*Callinectes sapidus*) that have shed their shell in order to grow a new one. They tend to hide themselves under rocks and

sand until the new shell grows, which is a quick process. Soft-shelled crabs are extremely delicate and do not keep or travel very well, so you will normally need to buy them frozen, although in the summer in the USA you can find fresh soft-shell crabs.

CRAYFISH various species including *Astacus fluviatilis*
Crayfish are also called crawfish or crawdad and are closely related to lobsters. Nearly all crayfish live in fresh water and most species are found in North America, particularly around Kentucky and Louisiana, although they are also found in Europe and throughout the world.

Crayfish are usually about 7cm (2¾in) long and have a joined head and midsection, a segmented body and eyes that are on moveable stalks. Their hard outer shell provides protection but does limit their growth. The smallest species of crayfish is about 2.5cm (1in) long and is found in southeast USA; the largest, which is found near Tasmania, reaches up to 40cm (16in) in length and can weigh 6kg (13lb).

Most crayfish live short lives – usually less than two years – so a high reproduction is important. The female crayfish can lay anything from 10 to 800 eggs, which will hatch in two to 20 weeks, depending on the temperature, and will stay attached until shortly after their second moult.

Crayfish have a wonderful flavour and, whatever their colour when alive (sandy yellow, green or dark brown), they turn a deep scarlet when cooked. Crayfish should ideally be bought live. There is a lot of wastage, so allow 8–12 per person. Keep the shells to make stock, soup or sauce.

LANGOUSTINES *Nephrops Norvegicus*

Otherwise known as Norway lobsters or Dublin Bay prawns, langoustines are usually around 20cm (8in) long and are, in effect, small lobsters. They are pale orange/pink in colour and the head and thorax have a non-segmented shell, while the long abdomen is segmented with a broad tan-like tail. Their eyes are large, black and immovable. The colder the water in which langoustines live, the better the flavour of the meat.

Langoustines deteriorate rapidly on being caught so are usually cooked and frozen at sea. If you do find them live, they need to be cooked soon after buying; make sure they are still moving. Place the live langoustines in a pan of cold water and bring them slowly to the boil. Boil for 4 minutes then transfer them to a bowl of iced water to cool.

Unlike other crustaceans, langoustines do not change colour when cooked. Clean langoustines in the same way as prawns, removing the black intestinal vein running down the back.

LOBSTERS

Lobsters are generally regarded as the finest crustaceans, as they have a firm, sweet flesh with a delicious flavour. They are also lower in saturated fat, cholesterol and calories than white chicken and so are very good for you as well as tasty.

Each of the lobster's eyes is set on a moveable stalk and has up to 10,000 facets, which operate like many tiny eyes. These make it possible for the lobsters to detect motion in dim light on the ocean floor. They also have tiny hairs that cover the body, including the legs, and these are sensitive to touch.

If a lobster likes what it picks up, it will pass the object to its mouth, where more hairs detect taste. It also has two strong claws, one for crushing and one for tearing the flesh, and it uses these claws for gripping and shredding food. It normally walks forward on its eight legs, but if threatened, it will contract its tail forcefully and move backwards quite rapidly.

Lobsters continue to grow throughout their lives, 'moulting' like crabs, but they grow very slowly, only reaching maturity at six years old. The lobsters normally served in restaurants weigh about 1kg (2lb 4oz) each, which means they are about 10 years old. This explains the short supply of lobsters and their high cost. The largest lobster ever caught weighed more than 20kg (44lb) and may have been 100 years old.

Lobsters must be alive when you cook them: a dead lobster is likely to give you extreme shellfish poisoning. Lobsters may be red, blue, albino or dark with yellow spots when alive, but all lobsters turn red on cooking. The quickest and most humane way to kill a lobster is to push a knife into the back of its head through the brain: this will kills it instantly.

CANADIAN/AMERICAN LOBSTER *Homarus Americanus*

These are found in large numbers around Canada and the North American Atlantic. They closely resemble the Scottish/European lobster but are greener and the claws are slightly fleshier than those of their European cousins. They do make excellent eating, but do not have the same quality of meat as the Scottish. Canadian/American lobsters are airfreighted live to Europe to try to meet the increasing demand for lobsters and the decreasing supply of Scottish lobsters. Even taking into the account the cost of shipping, them, they are still cheaper to buy in Europe than Scottish/European ones.

SCOTTISH/EUROPEAN LOBSTER *Homarus gammarus*

These lobsters are considered to have the best flavour of all lobsters. They are a blue black colour and may be dotted with bright blue spots. Scottish/European lobsters are becoming increasingly difficult to find and therefore very expensive. However, because of their superior quality, they are definitely worth the price if you can find them.

PRAWNS AND SHRIMP

Prawns and shrimp are very similar; in fact in the fish trade the names indicate only size: prawns less than 5cm (2in) are known as shrimp. In the USA, all are called shrimp.

Prawns and shrimp are scavengers, eating plankton and anything they can find on the ocean floor. They have quite a thin exoskeleton and their colour ranges from translucent brown, through greeny-grey to pink.

PINK SHRIMP *Pandalus montagui*

These are round-bodied prawns that grow up to 11cm (4½in) in length. They are translucent brownish in colour with variable markings, turning a lovely pink when cooked, and have a good flavour.

BROWN/COMMON SHRIMP *Crangon crangon*

These small shrimp are a grey colour and grow to only about 5cm (2in) in length. They turn a brownish colour once cooked and are quite fiddly to peel. You can eat them whole, but be warned that many have a lot of roe, which some people find unpalatable. These are the shrimp normally used to make potted shrimp; they are also great for soufflé.

MEDITERRANEAN OR KING PRAWNS family Penaeidae

These prawns can be as long as 10cm (4in) and vary in shades of red when caught; all will turn bright red once cooked. Mediterranean prawns are normally available to buy already cooked and ready to eat. They have a lovely texture and flavour.

TIGER PRAWNS *Penaeus esculentus*

A variety of king prawn, so called because of the striped banding around their body, tiger prawns are generally dark coloured with the rest of body being a light brown, blue or red. These are the largest commercially available prawns – they can grow up to 33cm (13in), which makes them ideal for the grill or barbecue. Tiger prawns have very succulent and firm flesh. They are available to buy frozen either in or out of the shell, but I prefer them in the shell, as this will impart a richer flavour to whatever you are cooking.

Molluscs

CLAMS numerous varieties

Clams feed upon plankton through a siphon, which acts like a snorkel. Within this are millions of little hairs that keep water circulating. Despite looking sturdy, clam shells are quite fragile and should be handled with care. All clams have a sweet flavour and a firm texture; most can either be cooked or eaten raw. Discard any with a broken shell or that is open before cooking as it may be dead and this will cause food poisoning. You should also discard any clam that remains closed once cooked.

PALOURDE *Tapes rhomboide* and *Tapes pullastra*

This is the most commonly available clam and the one that most people are familiar with. Palourdes are fairly small – 4–7cm (1½–2¾in) – with grooved brown shells with a yellow pattern. They can be very gritty so it is best to leave them in salted water overnight, changing the water a couple of times, to remove any sand or grit. They are very tender and can be eaten raw or cooked.

RAZOR CLAM *Ensis ensis*

These very strange-looking clams resemble an old-fashioned razor, with a long tube-like shell that is brown with some gold striping. The flesh tends to ooze out of the ends of the shells in a wormlike fashion. To ensure the clams are fresh, tap the shells and they should retract back into their shells. Often the look of these clams will put people off; if you are nervous, remove the flesh from the shell and chop it into pieces before eating it, but razor clams are worth trying for their delicious flavour.

AMERICAN CLAM *Mercenaria mercenaria*

These are often called 'cricket balls' in the fish markets due to their large size. American clams are very fleshy and do not lend themselves to being eaten raw as the meat can be quite tough. These clams also take longer to cook than their smaller cousins, but they do have a good flavour as well as a slightly meatier texture.

MUSSELS

Mussels attach themselves to rocks and each other using their beards (byssus) and can live in large congregations. Mussels feed on particles in the water, which is drawn in through a gap in the shell and expelled through an outflow tube.

BLACK-SHELL/COMMON MUSSELS

These coldwater mussels have a smooth bluish black shell, which looks pear shaped, and can grow up to 10cm (4in) long, although they are generally found at only half this size. Black-shell/common mussels are the most succulent of all mussels with a fairly sweet flavour. The female's flesh is a lovely orange colour, while the male has a lighter, cream-coloured flesh. Although some people maintain that the flesh of the female is better than that of the male, I do not think that there is much difference between the two.

OYSTERS

Oysters tend to evoke a strong response in most people – you either love them or hate them. I have to confess that they are not one of my favourite shellfish. They do, however, have a reputation as an aphrodisiac, which has helped increase their popularity. Unfortunately, it has also helped to decrease the stocks available. Because of centuries of over fishing and disease, most oysters are now cultivated and oyster cultivation has become highly profitable, even though it is a labour-intensive and very slow business. Rock oysters are grown for three years before being moved and 'fattened' for a year. As their name implies, native oysters grow wild and can take up to seven years to mature, hence their higher price.

Oysters feed by filtering food particles from the surrounding water:

the quantity of water pumped by a large, healthy oyster may approach 15 litres (4 gallons) an hour. Any matter brought into the oysters with the water is collected by mucus on the gills and large amounts of silt are discharged in this manner. (A pearl is the result of a tiny irritant, like a grain of sand, becoming imbedded in the oyster.)

Oysters are said to be in season when there is an 'r' in the month, but this applies only to wild oysters, which are protected from May to August, which is their breeding season. You can eat farmed oysters all year round.

NATIVE OYSTER *Ostrea edulis*

These are roundish in shape, generally a beige/grey shade to white, and are considered the best oysters and they are also the most expensive. Native oysters are normally named after their place of origin: for example, the Irish Galway and the English Whitstable.

ROCK OYSTER genus *Crassostrea*

Rock oysters are longer and rougher looking than the native ones, are often dark grey in colour and have rather coarse flesh. Although they are still good eaten raw in the traditional way, they lend themselves more to being cooked.

SCALLOPS family Pectinidae

Scallops are delicious molluscs – true treasures from the deep – though they are expensive. Venus is said to have emerged from the sea on a scallop shell and, no doubt as a result, scallops are believed by some to be an aphrodisiac.

Scallops are probably best known for their beautiful and distinctive scalloped shell, which is normally a salmon pink/orange colour. The edible part of the scallop is the white

muscle that opens and closes the two shells; this has a soft fleshy texture and a delicate flavour. The roe known as the 'coral' is also edible and is a bright orange in colour.

Unlike other bivalves (such as mussels and clams), scallops do not burrow in the sand or rocks, but rather swim above the sea bed by opening and closing their shells.

Scallops are primarily harvested by dredging, but this can cause them to become quite gritty. The best scallops are Diver scallops, which, as the name implies, are caught by people diving and collecting them.

Always take care not to overcook scallops as they become tough; as soon as they become white/opaque they are ready. Try to buy fresh scallops in the shell, otherwise buy the tubs of scallops 'dry' not 'wet'. The wet ones absorb too much water and do not have much flavour.

KING AND QUEEN SCALLOPS

Although they differ in size – the king (*Pecten maximus*) is larger than the queen (*Pecten opercularis*) – there is very little difference in flavour between them. Queen scallops are normally sold out of the shell and you need to allocate at least 10–12 per person as they are literally a mouthful. Because of their larger size, king scallops lend themselves better to ceviche, pan frying and baking.

WHELKS family Buccinidae

These marine snails have a whitish conical shell and are found on mud flats. They are particularly common on the coasts of the Atlantic and English Channel.

Whelks are best cooked for about 8–10 minutes in salted water – any longer and they become tough – and eaten with bread and butter or with mayonnaise or vinegar.

Thai prawn curry

Thai food happens to be one of my favourite foods – after Italian that is! And this recipe is one of my favourite Thai dishes – there's nothing better than eating this with your partner or family for a relaxing night at home. Enjoy!

SERVES: 4

Preparation time: 10 minutes
Cooking time: 45 minutes

1 teaspoon olive oil
1 garlic clove, finely chopped
5 shallots, finely chopped
2 tablespoons Thai green curry paste
3 tablespoons good fish stock
400ml (14fl oz) can coconut milk
20 raw tiger prawns, peeled and
   deveined
2 tablespoons chopped coriander
coconut rice to serve (optional)

method

1 Heat the olive oil in a pan and fry the garlic and shallots over a medium heat for 2 minutes. Stir in the Thai green curry paste and cook for a further 2 minutes, stirring continuously.

2 Add the fish stock and cook for 15 minutes over a medium heat, then stir in the coconut milk and cook for a further 15 minutes.

3 Add the prawns and cook for 10 minutes until the prawns are pink in colour. Stir in the chopped coriander and serve immediately, with coconut rice if desired.

BUTTERFLYING TIGER PRAWNS

1 Raw prawns are often peeled before cooking, but if you can, leave the shells on as they will add flavour to the prawns.

2 Insert a sharp knife just behind the head. Cut down the back all the way to the tail, so that the prawn is only attached at the head.

3 Using your fingers or a knife, pull out the black intestinal vein on one side. Repeat on the other side and then wash thoroughly.

4 These prawns are now butterflied and are ready for barbecuing, grilling or pan frying.

Prawn soufflé

This has to be one of the best recipes in the book! Don't be scared of making a soufflé – they are actually relatively easy. The main thing you need to ensure is that the ingredients are cold before you combine them.

SERVES: 4

Preparation time: 40 minutes
Cooking time: 35 minutes

1 tablespoon extra virgin olive oil
125g (4½oz) tiger prawns, peeled and cleaned
½ garlic clove, finely chopped
½ small red chilli, seeded and finely chopped
½ teaspoon finely chopped Italian flat-leaf parsley
dash vodka
salt and freshly ground black pepper
1 egg yolk
75ml (2½fl oz) double cream
2 egg whites, chilled
juice of ¼ lemon
butter to grease ramekins

Alternative shellfish:
lobster, crab

method

1 Heat the oil in a frying pan and add the prawns. Stir until they change colour, then add the chopped garlic, chilli and parsley. Deglaze the pan with the vodka and continue cooking for a further 3–4 minutes.

2 Remove the prawns from the pan and leave to cool to room temperature. (Make sure that they are completely cool before continuing; if they are too hot, the egg will begin to cook.) Place the cooled prawns in a food processor and blitz with a teaspoon of salt and the egg yolk until smooth. Refrigerate for 30 minutes.

3 Remove the mix from the fridge and transfer it into a stainless-steel bowl. Place the bowl into another bowl full of ice, then add the cream a little at a time, incorporating it at first by drizzling it from a spoon in small circles. Stir in a pinch of pepper and refrigerate again.

4 Preheat the oven to 160°C (325°F/gas 3).

5 In another large bowl, whisk the egg whites with a pinch of salt until they form stiff peaks, then carefully stir in the lemon juice.

6 Remove the prawn mixture from the fridge and, using a wooden spoon, mix it into the egg white using a fast circular motion until smooth.

7 Rub the insides of 4 individual ramekins with butter. Half fill them with the mixture. Place a sheet of greaseproof paper in a roasting pan to stop the ramekins from moving, then place the ramekins in the roasting pan, leaving plenty of space between each one. Fill the tray with hot water to a depth of 1.5cm (½in) and place in the oven. Cook the soufflés for 30 minutes until risen and golden brown. Serve immediately.

King prawns Portuguese style

When I'm in Portugal, I go out of my way to visit my favourite restaurant there. The food is amazing and the menu is full of mouthwatering fish dishes, which inspired me to come up with this one.

SERVES: 4

Preparation time: 10 minutes
Cooking time: 8 minutes

2 tablespoons olive oil
25g (1oz) unsalted butter
8 raw king prawns, cleaned and
   butterflied
6 garlic cloves, finely chopped
3 dry chillies, crushed
1 bunch spring onions, trimmed
   and finely chopped
3 tablespoons dry white wine
2 lemons
garlic bread to serve

method

1 Heat the oil and butter in a large frying pan, add the butterflied prawns and cook for 3–4 minutes until they become a nice pink colour.

2 Add the garlic, chilli and spring onions and cook for 3 minutes, then add the white wine and the juice of 1 lemon, continue cooking until half the liquid has evaporated.

3 Cut the other lemon into wedges. Serve the prawns with garlic bread and lemon wedges.

Alternative shellfish:
scallops, langoustines

Shrimp with brandy pâté

Pâté is normally associated with liver, but as I have a fish restaurant I tried making it with shrimp and really liked the result. This is a great recipe for a summer picnic – it's light and refreshing and it travels well.

SERVES: 4

Preparation time: 15 minutes plus
    2 hours marinating time

500g (1lb 2oz) cooked and peeled
    pink shrimp
2 tablespoons brandy
3 garlic cloves, peeled and finely
    chopped
pinch of paprika
1 teaspoon each salt and freshly
    ground black pepper
1 egg yolk
800g (1lb 12oz) butter, melted
3 tablespoons double cream
3 tiger prawns, cooked and peeled
3 lemon slices

method

1 Marinate the shrimp in the brandy, garlic and paprika for about 2 hours in the fridge.

2 Drain the shrimp, reserving the marinade, then blend in a food processor until smooth. Add salt and pepper, egg yolk and melted butter and process until butter is completely amalgamated.

3 Put the processor on a low speed and add 3 tablespoons of the marinade liquid and the cream. Blend until both have been absorbed into the mixture.

4 Line a terrine dish with cling film and pour the mixture into it. Level the top with a spatula and decorate with lemon slices and tiger prawns. Refrigerate for at least 30 minutes, then remove from the terrine dish by pulling the cling film.

Alternative shellfish:
white crab meat

Potted grey shrimp

This is quite an old-fashioned recipe but I really love it! There is a lot of butter in this recipe, but don't let this put you off – when you come to eat it, you can lift off the butter and eat only the shrimp.

SERVES: 4

Preparation time: 15 minutes
Cooking time: 10 minutes

225g (8oz) fresh brown/grey shrimp
1 teaspoon olive oil
350g (12oz) unsalted butter
1 bay leaf
½ teaspoon ground mace
salt and freshly ground black pepper
pinch of cayenne pepper
thin slices of brown toast to serve

method

1 Pan fry the shrimp in olive oil for about 3 minutes until cooked. Remove shrimp from the pan and set aside to cool, then peel them.

2 Melt 250g (9oz) of the butter in the pan and stir in the shrimp, bay leaf and ground mace and season with salt, black pepper and cayenne pepper. Cook over a low heat for 4 minutes. Discard the bay leaf and distribute the shrimp between 4 ramekins.

3 Clarify the remaining butter: cook it over a low heat until it is melted and foaming, then strain through muslin or cheesecloth. Completely cover the shrimp with the butter.

4 Leave to cool before refrigerating. Serve with thin slices of brown toast.

Right: Shrimp with brandy pâté

1 Holding the body of the langoustine with one hand, pull off the head with your other hand.

2 Holding the langoustine between your thumbs and forefingers, press down on the shell until it makes a cracking sound.

3 Turn the langoustine upside down and pull the shell away from the meat.

4 Pull the shell towards the tail and extract the meat. Remove the black intestinal vein running down the back.

Langoustine bisque

This is a more time-consuming recipe than most of the others in this book, but it is well worth the effort if you can make the time. Don't use frozen shellfish for this recipe as they will not give you the rich flavour you require.

SERVES: 4

Preparation time: 30 minutes
Cooking time: 1 hour

2.5kg (5lb 8oz) live langoustines
4 tablespoons olive oil
1 head of garlic, separated into
  cloves and peeled
1 head celery, peeled and diced
3 carrots, peeled and diced
1 onion, peeled and chopped
1 leek, peeled and chopped
2 tablespoons brandy
2.5 litres (4½ pints) fish stock
2 tablespoons tomato purée
10 black peppercorns
1 tablespoon sea salt
1 bunch fresh parsley

method

1 Put the live langoustines in cold water and bring them slowly to the boil. Boil for 4 minutes, then transfer them to a bowl of iced water to cool.

2 Prepare the langoustines following the steps above. Reserve the shells and chop the meat.

3 In a large sauté pan, heat the oil and garlic until smoking. Add the langoustine shells and cook for 4–5 minutes, then add the celery, carrots, onion and leek and cook for 2 minutes. Deglaze the pan with the brandy and fish stock, then stir in the tomato purée, peppercorns and sea salt.

4 Bring back to the boil and skim off any fat, then simmer, uncovered, for 40–45 minutes, skimming again if necessary. Add most of the parsley leaves, reserving some for garnish, and continue simmering until the liquid has reduced by half.

5 Pass the bisque through a sieve then strain through 2 layers of damp muslin. Return the liquid to a gentle boil then stir in the langoustine meat.

6 Serve the bisque in large bowls with parsley leaves scattered on top and a drizzle of extra virgin olive oil.

Alternative shellfish:
lobster, shrimp

Grilled langoustines

I love langoustines: they are really delicate with a sweet, distinct flavour. This is a fantastic way to cook them – a really simple recipe but full of flavour.

Alternative shellfish:
prawns, scallops

SERVES: 4

Preparation time: 10 minutes plus
   1 hour marinating time
Cooking time: 5 minutes

16 prepared langoustines
1 fresh chilli, seeded and chopped
2 garlic cloves, crushed
juice of 1 lemon
1 teaspoon crushed sea salt
1 tablespoon extra virgin olive oil
tartar sauce or sweet chilli sauce
   and salad to serve

method

1 Marinate the prepared langoustines in the chilli, garlic, lemon juice, salt and oil.

2 Place under a hot grill and cook for 5 minutes.

3 Serve with tartar sauce or sweet chilli sauce and salad.

1 Put the flour on a work surface, make a well in the centre and add the eggs, oil and salt.

2 Mix in a circular motion, slowly incorporating the flour into the egg mixture.

3 Knead for 5 minutes, adding extra flour to the surface until the dough is elastic and springs back when gently pressed.

4 Using either a pasta machine or a rolling pin, roll out all the pasta dough on a floured surface, fold over lengthways in half, mark a point at the crease and unfold again.

SERVES: 4

Preparation time: 45 minutes plus 30 minutes resting
Cooking time: 45 minutes

Ravioli dough
400g (14oz) 00 flour
4 eggs
30ml (2 tablespoons) olive oil
75ml (5 tablespoons) cold water
a pinch of salt
extra flour for dusting

Crayfish filling
800g crayfish, cooked, shelled and the meat finely chopped (reserve the shells and pound them)
60ml (4 tablespoons) mascarpone
15ml (1 tablespoon) chopped fresh flat-leaf parsley
6 fresh basil leaves, shredded

Sauce
45ml (3 tablespoons) olive oil
30g (1oz) butter
1 small onion, finely chopped
1 stick celery, trimmed and finely chopped
1 small carrot, finely chopped
1 fat garlic clove, crushed
30g (1oz) plain flour
15ml (1 tablespoon) tomato purée
60ml (2fl oz) brandy
300ml (10fl oz) good fish stock
600ml (1 pint) double cream
salt and freshly ground black pepper

Crayfish ravioli

This great shellfish is quite versatile, mostly used for soups, stocks and sauces but my ravioli has been a huge success in Zilli Fish so I wanted to share the experience with you.

method

1 Make the pasta dough using Steps 1 to 3 above. Cover dough with cling film and allow to rest for 30 minutes.

2 Meanwhile, mix together all the filling ingredients and season to taste. Set aside.

3 For the sauce: heat the oil in a heavy-based pan, add the butter and heat until melted. Stir in the onion, celery, carrot, garlic and cook over a very low heat for 10 minutes until soft. Add the pounded shells, flour and tomato purée and cook, stirring well, for a further 5 minutes.

4 Put the brandy in a large metal ladle or small pan and ignite, then pour over the vegetables. Once the flames die down, stir in the stock and cream. Cook over a low heat for 20 minutes until reduced to a coating consistency. Pass through a fine sieve and return it to a clean pan. Season to taste and set aside.

5 Fill the ravioli while the sauce is cooking.

6 Bring a large pan of salted water to a rolling boil. Add the ravioli in batches. Once the ravioli rise to the surface, cook for 1 minute more, drain and place in the pan of crayfish lobster sauce. Shake the pan gently to coat the ravioli with the sauce and serve immediately.

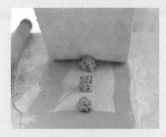   

5 Spoon walnut-sized scoops of the crayfish filling on to one-half of the pasta at 2.5cm (1in) intervals.

6 Brush the edges with an egg wash then fold over the other leaf of pasta and seal around the filling using your fingertips.

7 Cut out the ravioli either in squares or by using a round pastry cutter.

8 Crimp the edges with a fork. The ravioli is now ready to be added to salted boiling water.

Seafood risotto

Risotto and fish is a great combination! You can choose whatever fish you like for this dish; just make sure you use a good fish stock. Add stock to the risotto gradually: if you add too much you will end up with soup instead.

SERVES: 4

Preparation time: 30 minutes
Cooking time: 30 minutes

1.5 litres (2¾ pints) fish stock
85g (3oz) butter
1 medium onion, finely chopped
2 garlic cloves, finely chopped
1 bay leaf, torn in half
350g (12oz) risotto rice
225g (8oz) mussels, scrubbed, beards and barnacles removed
150ml (5fl oz) white wine such as Prosecco
175g (6oz) firm fish fillet (e.g. cod, salmon, haddock), skinned and cut into 5cm (2in) pieces
2 tablespoons chopped fresh parsley
1 tablespoon chopped chives
salt and freshly ground black pepper

method

1 Pour the stock into a large pan and bring to a gentle simmer.

2 Meanwhile, melt 25g (1oz) of the butter in a large pan, add the onion, garlic and 2 bay leaf halves and sauté for 5–8 minutes until soft. Stir in the rice. Cook, stirring, for about 30 seconds.

3 Gradually add the stock, a ladleful at a time, to the rice, stirring and adding more stock as each batch is absorbed. The total cooking time will be about 20 minutes, at the end of which the rice should be *al dente*. Season well to taste. Set aside.

4 Meanwhile, place the mussels in a separate pan, add the wine, cover tightly and cook over a high heat for 3–5 minutes, shaking the pan frequently, until the shells have opened. Strain the pan juices through a fine sieve and reserve. Discard any mussels that have remained closed.

5 Return the risotto to a low heat and stir in the remaining butter. Add some of the reserved pan juices if the risotto is a little dry. Stir in the fish, mussels, parsley and chives and season to taste. Cook for a further 1–2 minutes until the fish is tender and just flakes. Discard the bay leaf halves.

6 Spoon the risotto into 4 large warmed bowls, sprinkle with black pepper and serve immediately.

Crayfish salad with mango and citrus dressing

If you like crayfish, you will enjoy this great summer salad. When mixing leaves and dressing together, put the dressing in a stainless-steel bowl, then add the rest of the ingredients and toss gently to ensure an even coating.

SERVES: 4

Preparation time: 15 minutes

1 egg yolk
1 teaspoon English mustard
6 tablespoons olive oil
juice of 1 orange
juice of 1 lemon
juice of 1 lime
200g (7oz) baby spinach leaves
40g (1½oz) toasted croutons
400g (14oz) crayfish meat
2 mangoes, peeled and diced
1 pinch of paprika
salt and freshly ground black pepper

Alternative shellfish:
crab, shrimp

method

1 In a large stainless steel bowl, whisk the egg yolk and mustard together. Add the oil a little at a time, whisking continuously, until you have a mayonnaise-like consistency. Gently whisk in the orange, lemon and lime juices.

2 In another bowl, mix together the baby spinach, croutons and half the dressing until the leaves and croutons are evenly coated.

3 Mix the crayfish with the remaining dressing, half the mango and the paprika and make sure it is well coated. Season to taste.

4 Place the spinach leaves in a pile on each plate, top with the crayfish mix and scatter over remaining mango before serving.

PREPARING LOBSTER

1 Place the lobster on a board and pierce the centre of the head with a sharp knife to kill it.

2 Pull the knife towards the tail in a smooth action. Cut through the tail.

3 Cut through the head so that you end up with 2 lobster halves.

4 Using the back of a knife, smash the claws a couple of times. This will make it easier for you to remove the meat from them.

Lobster thermidor

There are lots of variations of this dish but this is the way I cook it and my customers seem to love it! Make sure that you use live lobsters as this will provide the best result. I introduced my daughter, Laura, to shellfish with this dish.

SERVES: 4

Preparation time: 20 minutes
Cooking time: 5 minutes

2 live lobsters (400–500g/
   14oz–1lb 2oz each), boiled for
   5 minutes only
150g (5½oz) butter
16 spring onions, finely chopped
2 tablespoons plain flour
2 teaspoons English mustard
4 tablespoons white wine
250ml (9fl oz) milk
4 tablespoons double cream
2 tablespoons finely chopped
   parsley
salt and freshly ground black pepper
115g (4oz) cheese (Parmesan,
   Dolcelatte, Stilton or Gruyère)

method

1 Using a sharp knife, cut the lobster in half lengthways. Lift the meat from the tail and the body. Crack the claws and prise the meat from them. Remove the intestinal vein and discard. Cut the meat into bite-sized pieces, cover and refrigerate. Wash the lobster shell, drain and dry.

2 Heat 55g (2oz) of the butter in a frying pan and cook the spring onions for 2 mintues. Add the flour and the mustard and cook for a further 1 minute. Remove from the heat and gradually add the wine and the milk. Return to the heat and cook, stirring continuously to avoid any lumps, until the mixture has thickened.

3 Stir in the cream, parsley and lobster meat and season; heat gently. Spoon this mixture into the lobster shells, sprinkle with cheese and dot with the remaining butter.

4 Place under a preheated grill and cook for 2 minutes, or until the top is lightly browned.

Alternative shellfish:
king prawns

Spaghetti with fresh lobster

My signature dish in all of my restaurants and it has been for 10 years, since the day the fishmonger delivered 20 lobsters by mistake! The chef and I came up with this great recipe and it has been a success with visitors to the restaurant, including the local media set and celebs, ever since! Make sure that you always start with a live lobster as it makes all the difference to the flavour.

SERVES: 2

Preparation time: 30 minutes
Cooking time: 15 minutes

175g (6oz) spaghetti
fresh basil sprigs to garnish

Sauce
1 x 900g (2lb) live lobster
2 beef tomatoes, skinned and
    seeded
60ml (4 tablespoons) freshly
    chopped flat-leaf parsley
60ml (4 tablespoons) freshly
    chopped basil
2 garlic cloves, peeled and finely
    chopped
salt and freshly ground black pepper
    50ml (2fl oz) olive oil
1 small red onion, peeled and finely
    chopped
50ml (2fl oz) brandy
150ml (5fl oz) dry white wine

method

1 Place the lobster in the freezer for about 15 minutes, then put directly into salted boiling water and cook for 5 minutes until the shell turns pink. Remove from the water and set aside to cool.

2 Split the lobster in half lengthways and break off the claws. Wash the inside of the lobster to remove the innards. Gently remove the lobster meat from the shells, trying to keep the claw meat intact; chop the body meat. Wash the lobster body shells and set aside to use for presentation.

3 Chop the tomato flesh and place in a bowl with the parsley, basil and half of the garlic. Season with salt and freshly ground black pepper. Set aside.

4 In a large frying pan heat half of the oil and add the onion and remaining garlic. Cook for two minutes and pour over the brandy; ignite the alcohol to flambé. Once the flames have died down add the tomato mixture and lobster meat with the wine. Simmer for 5–8 minutes until the juices reduce slightly.

5 Meanwhile bring a large pan of salted water to the boil. Add the spaghetti and cook for 5-8 minutes, or according to the instructions on the packet, until al dente. Drain and add to the lobster sauce, tossing well to mix. Adjust the seasoning if necessary.

6 If using the lobster shells for presentation, place on 2 large serving plates or bowls and top with the spaghetti, spooning over sauce. Drizzle over the remaining oil, garnish with basil sprigs and serve immediately.

Lobster in Grand Marnier and kumquat sauce

Cooking lobster this way really brings out its flavour. Again, please be sure to find live lobsters as this will make all the difference to the taste. If you can't find kumquats, clementines or oranges will work just as well.

SERVES: 4

Preparation time: 10 minutes
Cooking time: 15 minutes

4 live lobsters (400–500g/14oz–
    1lb 2oz each)
salt and freshly ground black pepper
2 tablespoons extra virgin olive oil
55g (2oz) unsalted butter
4 shallots, finely chopped
4 garlic cloves, finely chopped
2 teaspoons chopped coriander
2 teaspoons brown sugar
12 kumquats, peeled
3 tablespoons Grand Marnier

method

1 Cook the live lobsters for 5 minutes until pink. Open the lobster by cutting in half lengthways and remove the green intestinal vein. Preheat the oven to 190°C (375°F/gas 5).

2 Season the lobster with salt and pepper and 2 tablespoons of olive oil and place under the grill, shell side up, for 5 minutes until the meat is marked by the grill lines.

3 In a large frying pan heat the butter, shallots, garlic, coriander, sugar and kumquats. Cook the fruit until it is glistening and the sugar has caramelized the fruit, then add the Grand Marnier and 1 cup of water.

4 Pour the sauce and fruit over the lobster and cook in the oven for 10 minutes. Place a lobster half on each of 4 individual plates and pour over the sauce.

Alterative fish:
king prawns

Lobster burgers with chilli relish

Burgers or fish cakes are normally made with inexpensive fish or shellfish but if you really fancy a treat then this is the one for you. You can, of course, serve the burger in a roll – an alternative version of fast food!

SERVES: 4

Preparation time: 10 minutes
Cooking time: 9 minutes

500g (1lb 2oz) fresh lobster meat
40g (1½oz) rice flour or cornflour
1 small red chilli, seeded and finely
    chopped
2 garlic cloves, finely chopped
2 spring onions, finely chopped
2 teaspoons finely chopped Italian
    flat-leaf parsley
2 egg yolks
1 teaspoon soy sauce
salt and freshly ground black pepper
4 salad leaves
chilli relish
fat chips to serve

method

1 Preheat the oven to 180°C (350°F/gas 4).

2 In a large bowl, place the lobster meat, flour, chilli, garlic, spring onions, parsley, egg yolks and soy sauce, season with salt and pepper and stir together with your hands until the mixture is smooth and your fingers are dry.

3 Divide the mixture into 4 equal portions, roll into balls and flatten slightly with the palm of your hand to form burgers.

4 Heat the grill and sear the burgers on each side. Transfer to a baking sheet and finish in the oven for about 6 minutes. Serve on top of the salad leaves, with chilli relish and fat chips.

Right: Lobster burgers with chilli relish

PREPARING CRAB

1 Lay the crab upside down on a chopping board.

2 Insert a sharp knife between the mouth plates and the eyes of the crab.

3 Using the knife as a lever, remove the top shell, which will remove the inside of the crab.

4 You will end up with a shell that resembles that of a scallop. Pull off the claws.

5 This is how the crab should look once you have taken it all apart.

6 Using the back of the knife, smash the claws to get at the meat. (You may want to cover the claws with a cloth as this can be messy.)

7 Once you have cracked the claw, the meat will come out in one piece with only a thin 'plastic' piece in the middle of the meat.

8 Using a spoon, remove the brown meat from the shell, making sure that you scoop out all the solid brown meat from the sides.

Creole crab

This is a very good recipe for crab, with lots of flavour. For an alternative dish, place the crab in ramekins, sprinkle with 55g (2oz) each of breadcrumbs and butter and cook in the oven at 180°C (350°F/gas 4) for 10 minutes.

SERVES: 6

Preparation time: 15 minutes

400g (14oz) white crab meat
3 eggs, hard boiled and shelled
1 teaspoon wholegrain mustard
3 tablespoons extra virgin olive oil
pinch of cayenne pepper
pinch of paprika
2 tablespoons sherry
2 tablespoons chopped parsley
115ml (4fl oz) single cream
3 spring onions, finely sliced
salt and freshly ground black pepper
6 tomatoes, sliced, to serve
6 sprigs basil to garnish

method

1 Make sure your crab meat has been well picked and there is no shell or cartilage in the meat. Flake the meat into a bowl, if possible keeping the pieces fairly large.

2 Remove the egg yolks from the hard-boiled eggs, place in a bowl and crumble them with a fork. Add the mustard, oil, cayenne pepper and paprika and mash until you form a paste, then stir in the sherry and the parsley.

3 Chop the egg whites and add them to the yolk mixture with the cream and spring onions. Mix well and then gently fold in the crab meat. Season to taste and serve immediately with sliced tomatoes and garnished with basil.

Crab claws pan fried with pesto

As crabs tend to lose their claws, most fishmongers will have some to buy, so you don't need to get the whole crab. You can adjust this recipe and make the claws with garlic, chilli and olive oil if you prefer. Either way, this is a wonderful meal. The pesto can be kept for up to a week as long as it is covered with olive oil.

SERVES: 4

Preparation time: 10 minutes
Cooking time: 6 minutes

4 tablespoons extra virgin olive oil
12 large crab claws, cracked but
    still in the shell
8 garlic cloves
2 teaspoons chopped Italian
    flat-leaf parsley
5 tablespoons dry white wine
toasted ciabatta to serve

Pesto
85g (3oz) Pecorino, freshly grated
25g (1oz) Parmesan, freshly grated
25g (1oz) fresh basil leaves
15g (½oz) sun-dried tomatoes
2 tablespoons toasted pine nuts
2 garlic cloves, finely chopped
250ml (9fl oz) extra virgin olive oil
salt and freshly ground black pepper

method

1 First make the pesto: blitz all the ingredients together in a food processor. If you are not using it straight away, ensure that the pesto is covered with olive oil.

2 Heat the oil in a large frying pan, then add the crab claws, garlic and the parsley. Cook for 2 minutes until the garlic is a golden colour, stirring occasionally.

3 Add the wine and pesto to the pan and cook for 4 minutes. Serve hot with thin slices of toasted ciabatta.

Crab and vegetable frittata

Fritatta is the Italian version of the omelette and is probably the most versatile dish to make with eggs. I find it marries very well with shellfish as well as with vegetables and cheese. I remember tasting this particular one in Soho, New York, and I thought I'd share it with you.

SERVES: 4

Preparation time: 10 minutes
Cooking time: 25 minutes

8 eggs
1 tablespoon double cream
salt and ground black pepper
1 red onion, finely chopped
2 courgettes, diced
1 red pepper, diced
1 yellow pepper, diced
1 tablespoon olive oil
100g (3½oz) white crab meat
1 tablespoon chopped parsley
mixed leaf salad to serve

method

1 Whisk the eggs together with the double cream and season. Preheat the oven to 190°C (375°F/gas 5).

2 Pan fry the onion, courgettes and peppers for 3 minutes in olive oil, then add the crab meat and continue cooking for a further 3 minutes.

3 Line an ovenproof dish with greaseproof paper and lay the vegetable and crab mixture along the bottom of the dish. Pour over the egg mixture and cook in the oven for 10–15 minutes until the egg has risen and is golden brown. Remove and set aside to cool completely. Sprinkle with chopped parsley.

4 Serve the frittata, cut into wedges, with a mixed leaf salad.

Alternative fish:
lobster, scallop or prawn meat

Spider crab with linguine and courgettes

While spider crabs are not the most attractive looking of shellfish, their meat is a lot sweeter than that of Common crab and it makes this sauce very tasty. You can, of course, use other crabs for this recipe if you prefer.

SERVES: 4

Preparation time: 30 minutes plus 20 minutes cooling time
Cooking time: 50 minutes

4 medium live spider crabs (450g/1lb each)
160ml (5½fl oz) extra virgin olive oil
1 bunch of spring onions, finely chopped
6 garlic cloves, finely chopped
2 red chillies, finely chopped
500g (1lb 2oz) linguine
3 courgettes, diced
2 tablespoons finely chopped Italian flat-leaf parsley
4 tablespoons white wine
juice of 1 lemon

Alternative fish:
Common crab

method

1 Preheat the oven to 180°C (350°F/gas 4). Place the crabs in a large pot of cold water and bring slowly to the boil. Cook for 20 minutes, then cool in a large bowl of iced water for about 20 minutes.

2 Remove the meat from the crabs, reserving the crab shells. Crack the claws, place them in a roasting tray with 100ml (3½fl oz) olive oil, half the spring onions, half the garlic and 1 chilli and roast in the oven for 16 minutes.

3 Meanwhile, cook the pasta according to the packet instructions, draining it 1 minute before the end of the recommended cooking time.

4 In a frying pan, heat the remaining extra virgin olive oil, garlic, chilli and spring onions and the courgettes. Stir, cook for 2 minutes, then add the crab meat and 1 tablespoon of parsley. Deglaze the pan with the white wine and add the linguine. Sauté the pasta and crab for 1 minute, add lemon juice and stir.

5 Using tongs, remove the pasta and crab meat from the pan and divide between the crab shells. Remove the claws from the oven and set alongside the body. Sprinkle with remaining parsley and serve immediately.

PREPARING MUSSELS

1 Make sure none of the mussels is open, as this means they are either dead or full of sand. Discard any open mussels.

2 Using a knife remove the 'beard' from all the mussels; you will need to pull some of this out.

3 Place the mussels in a bowl of clean salted water and leave overnight to remove any sand or grit. Change the water at least twice.

Adriatic fish stew

Stew is not really quite the word to describe this dish, but soup doesn't work either. Whatever you decide to call it, however, this is a favourite recipe of mine and a dish that I eat every time I am in Italy.

SERVES: 6

Preparation time: 20 minutes
Cooking time: 50 minutes

400g (14oz) whole small fish (e.g. mackerel, red mullet, sea bream)
500g (1lb 2oz) fish fillets (e.g. sole, sea bass, cod, grey or red mullet)
300g (10½oz) small squid
400g (14oz) fresh mussels in shells
300g (10½oz) raw prawns
1 onion, peeled and cut into quarters
1 carrot, peeled and cut into quarters
2 sticks celery, peeled and chopped
6 garlic cloves
625ml (22½fl oz) dry white wine
400g (14oz) ripe plum tomatoes
5 tablespoons extra virgin olive oil
2 red chillies, seeded and chopped
pinch of saffron strands
salt and freshly ground black pepper
25g (1oz) Italian flat-leaf parsley, chopped

method

1 Gut and scale the whole fish, if your fishmonger hasn't already done so. Wash thoroughly in running water and cut off the heads. Cut the fillets into 2.5cm (1in) pieces.

2 Trim and rinse the squid and cut into 1cm (½in) wide rings. Wash and scrape the mussels and discard any that are open. Wash and shell the prawns, removing any dark vein-like intestines.

3 Place the onion, carrot, celery, mushrooms, 3 whole garlic cloves (peeled) and whole small fish in a pan and cover with 1 litre (1¾ pints) of cold, slightly salted water. Bring to the boil, then immediately reduce the heat and simmer for 20 minutes.

4 Meanwhile heat a heavy-based pan, place the cleaned mussels inside, cover and cook for 2–3 minutes until they begin to open. Add 125ml (4½fl oz) of white wine and cook until all the mussels are cooked and open. (Discard any that remain closed.) Strain the mussel stock and remove the mussels from their shells (leaving 8 in the shell for garnish). Add the mussel stock to the fish stock and keep mussels to one side.

5 Peel and chop the tomatoes and the remaining 3 garlic cloves. Pour the extra virgin olive oil into a large pan, add the chopped garlic, tomatoes, cleaned squid, shelled prawns and chopped chillies. Stir in 500ml (18fl oz) of white wine, cover the pan and simmer for 15 minutes. Add the saffron strands and salt and pepper to taste.

6 Remove the whole fish from the stock and separate the fish from the bones. Discard the bones and add the fish to the tomato sauce.

7 Add the fish fillets, stock and mussels to the tomato sauce and correct the seasoning. Serve garnished with chopped parsley and the reserved mussels in the shell.

Mussels diablo

This is a spicy dish but is great for the day after a few drinks. Adjust the amount of chilli to suit your own taste and serve lots of lovely crusty bread to dip into the sauce.

SERVES: 4

Preparation time: 10 minutes
Cooking time: 20–25 minutes

1.5kg (3lb 8oz) mussels, cleaned
2 tablespoons olive oil
3 garlic cloves, finely chopped
6 red chillies, seeded and finely
    chopped
2 tablespoons Italian flat-leaf
    parsley, finely chopped
250ml (9fl oz) dry white wine
425g (15oz) canned chopped
    tomatoes (or passata)
toasted ciabatta to serve

method

1 Discard any mussels that are open. Heat half the oil in a large pan and add the mussels, garlic, chilli and half the parsley. Cover and simmer over medium heat for 4–5 minutes.

2 After 4 minutes, begin to remove mussels that have opened; after 6 minutes, remove and discard any that have not opened.

3 Clean the pan, heat the remaining oil and add mussels, wine and chopped tomatoes or passata. Cook for 15 minutes. Stir in the remainder of the parsley.

4 Serve the mussels hot in bowls with toasted sliced ciabatta.

Mussels with herb breadcrumbs, gratinated

I love mussels in lots of different ways but I find this to be very tasty and it also works very well with clams. If you wish, you can add pesto to the breadcrumbs, which will give a lovely flavour to the mussels.

SERVES: 4

Preparation time: 10 minutes
Cooking time: 6 minutes

300g (10½oz) white breadcrumbs
2 tablespoons fresh basil leaves
2 tablespoons Italian flat-leaf parsley
2 tablespoons finely chopped lemon
   thyme
2 garlic cloves
2 marinated anchovies
salt and freshly ground black pepper
40g (1½oz) unsalted butter
4 tablespoons extra virgin
   olive oil
20 large mussels,
   open in the ½ shell
lemon wedges and
   salad to serve

method

1 Preheat the grill. In a food processor, blend the breadcrumbs, basil, parsley, lemon thyme, garlic, anchovies, salt and pepper until the crumbs are light green in colour, then add the butter and the olive oil.

2 Fill each mussel with some of the breadcrumb mixture and place the mussels on a baking tray. Cook under the preheated grill for about 5–6 minutes until brown and crispy. Serve hot with lemon wedges and salad.

Alternative shellfish:
clams

Razor clams with Oriental herbs and noodles

Razor clams are not very well known, but I have to say I love them. This Oriental-inspired recipe brings out their great flavour and looks impressive on the plate.

SERVES: 4

Preparation time: 10 minutes
Cooking time: 18 minutes

4 tablespoons sesame oil
2 red chillies, chopped
4 garlic cloves, finely sliced
1 teaspoon chopped fresh root
    ginger
12 large razor clams, washed
150g (5½oz) bean sprouts
100g (3½oz) green beans, sliced
450g (1lb) egg noodles, cooked in
    boiling water until tender
2 tablespoons soy sauce
1 tablespoon oyster sauce
salt and freshly ground black pepper
1 bunch spring onions, finely
    chopped
2 tablespoons chopped coriander

method

1 Preheat the oven to 140°C (275°F/gas 1). Heat 2 tablespoons of the sesame oil in a wok and stir-fry half the chillies, half the garlic and half the ginger for 1–2 minutes. Add the clams, cover and cook until the clams have opened. Discard any clams that remain unopened.

2 Remove the clams from the wok, place in a roasting pan and bake in the oven for 10 minutes.

3 Meanwhile, in the same wok, heat the remaining oil and add remaining garlic, chilli and ginger along with the bean sprouts and green beans. Stir fry for 2 minutes, then stir in the noodles, soy sauce and oyster sauce and continue cooking for a further 4 minutes. Season to taste.

4 Using tongs, place the noodles on each of 4 plates, arrange 3 clams on top of each pile of noodles and pour over any remaining juices. Scatter over the chopped spring onions and coriander and serve immediately.

Alternative shellfish:
palourdes

Clams in their own juice

This is the best way of cooking clams, when they're fresh and full of flavour. A lot of people add wine to this dish, but I think that it spoils the taste of the clams; with water they retain the freshness of the sea.

SERVES: 4

Preparation time: 10 minutes
Cooking time: 10 minutes

100ml (3½fl oz) extra virgin olive oil
55g (2oz) shallots, finely chopped
2 garlic cloves, crushed
½ chilli, seeded and finely chopped
800g (1lb 12oz) clams, washed

100ml (3½fl oz) water
150g (5½oz) cherry tomatoes, halved
200ml (7fl oz) fish stock
3 tablespoons finely chopped parsley
salt and freshly ground black pepper
bruschetta to serve

method

1 Heat the oil in a large heavy-based saucepan and add the shallots, garlic and chilli. Cook for 1 minute and add the clams. Cover the pan and cook for 2 minutes, then add the water. Cook for a further 2 minutes, shaking the pan occasionally.

2 Add the cherry tomatoes, fish stock and parsley and continue cooking for a further 5 minutes. If any clams are not open, tap with a spoon; if they still do not open, remove and discard. Season to taste and then serve in a large bowl with some bruschetta.

Large American clam hot pot

Large clams are normally quite tough but cooked this way they are lovely and tender. If you are using smaller clams, reduce the cooking time or they will become tough.

SERVES: 4

Preparation time: 10 minutes plus
   2–3 hours soaking time
Cooking time: 15 minutes

2kg (4lb 8oz) large fresh clams
2 tablespoons olive oil
4 garlic cloves, finely chopped
4 shallots, finely chopped
225ml (8fl oz) double cream
salt and freshly ground black pepper
1 teaspoon finely chopped chives

method

1 Wash and scrub the clams and place in a large plastic container filled with water and add a good pinch of salt. Leave them for 2–3 hours to remove any sand or grit in the clams. Discard any clams that are open.

2 Heat the olive oil in a large pan, add the garlic and shallots and cook for 30 seconds. Add the clams and, using a wooden spoon to stir and turn them, cook for 1 minute on each side. Add the cream, a pinch of salt and some black pepper and cook for a further 10–15 minutes, or until all the clams are open – you may need to add a little water during this time.

3 Place the clams in a large bowl, discarding any that have not opened, and cover with the sauce. Sprinkle with the chives and serve immediately.

Right: Large American clam hot pot

PREPARING SCALLOPS

1 It is best to use diver scallops if possible as dredged scallops can contain a lot of grit.

2 Grasp hold of the scallop and insert the knife between the two halves of the shell. Twist the knife slightly to make a wider gap.

3 Run the blade along the inner shell to cut through the ligament that joins the meat to the shell.

4 Open up the scallop and lift off the top half of the shell.

Diver scallops St Jacques

This is a very old recipe but none the less a very tasty one. The choice of cheese you use is entirely up to you, although I would stay away from really strong cheeses or you will lose the flavour of the scallops.

SERVES: 4

Preparation time: 10 minutes
Cooking time: 10 minutes

175ml (6fl oz) dry white wine
1 bay leaf
4 peppercorns
1 onion, finely chopped
25g (1oz) butter
1½ tablespoons flour
175ml (6fl oz) milk
salt and freshly ground black pepper
25g (1oz) fontina cheese, finely
   diced
1 teaspoon Dijon mustard
12 scallops on the ½ shell
2 tablespoons dry breadcrumbs
25g (1oz) grated Parmesan cheese

method

1 Place the wine, bay leaf, peppercorns and onion in a small pan and bring to the boil, then reduce the heat and simmer until the liquid has reduced by three quarters. Strain the liquid and set aside.

2 Melt the butter in a small pan and add the flour, cook for 1 minute, stirring continuously, then remove from the heat and gradually stir in the milk and the wine reduction, stirring until smooth. Return the pan to the heat and continue stirring until the mixture thickens. Season with salt and black pepper, then add the fontina cheese and the mustard.

3 Preheat the grill. Spoon this mixture over the scallops and sprinkle with breadcrumbs and Parmesan. Cook under the grill until crisp and golden brown and serve immediately.

5 Slide the knife under the scallop and remove any muscle.

6 Remove and discard the frilly orangey-grey intestine underneath the scallop and the black intestine, which runs along the side.

7 Trim the scallop and you should end up with a clean white scallop and a bright orange roe.

Scallop ceviche with chilli, spring onions and soy

Scallops are a great shellfish to eat raw, but make sure they are absolutely fresh. You can use other scallops for this dish but divers work best as they tend not to have any grit or sand in them.

SERVES: 4

Preparation time: 15 minutes
    plus 1 hour chilling time

12 fresh diver scallops, prepared
sea salt
juice of 1 lime
juice of ½ lemon
extra virgin olive oil
1 garlic clove, finely chopped
2 red chillies, seeded and finely
    chopped
1 bunch coriander, chopped
6 spring onions, chopped
4 tablespoons soy sauce

method

1 Thinly slice the scallops and place them in a wide, flat-bottomed dish.

2 Sprinkle with sea salt, then pour over lime and lemon juice, cover with extra virgin olive oil and then add the garlic, chilli, coriander and spring onions. Leave in the fridge for 1 hour. (The longer you leave it the more the flavours will be absorbed by the scallops.)

3 For presentation, place the thin slices of scallops on 4 clean dry scallop shells, drizzle with the soy sauce and serve.

Pan-fried scallops

Scallops are one of those shellfish that eveyone loves. They are best cooked very simply and really don't need anything to add flavour to them as they have such an amazing taste of their own.

SERVES: 4

Preparation time: 10 minutes
Cooking time: 2 minutes

4 tablespoons balsamic vinegar
1 teaspoon sea salt
12 scallops, cleaned and roe
    removed
250g (9oz) baby spinach leaves
    to serve

method

1 Heat the balsamic vinegar in a pan until reduced by half.

2 Place a grill pan on top of the stove and heat until very hot. Sprinkle the grill pan with the sea salt and sear the scallops for 1 minute on each side. (The salt prevents the scallops from sticking to the pan.)

3 Pile some baby spinach leaves in the centre of each plate and surround with 3 scallops per portion. Pour the balsamic reduction on top of the spinach leaves.

Pea, mint and scallop risotto

Risotto has become a very popular dish in England as it can be made with pretty much any seasonal ingredients but not that often with fish or seafood. One of my favourite recipes is with lobster or crab but with this recipe scallops give it a lovely delicate and luxurious taste to compliment the mint and peas, so enjoy.

SERVES: 4

Preparation time: 10 minutes
Cooking time: 50 minutes

1.5 litres chicken stock
85g butter
1 medium onion, finely diced
2 garlic cloves, finely diced
2 bay leaves, torn in half
300g Arborio risotto rice
16–20 scallops, cleaned
150ml Prosecco
100g peas
5 tablespoons chopped fresh mint
2 tablespoons chopped fresh
  parsley
1 tablespoon chopped fresh chives
salt and freshly ground black pepper

method

1 Pour the stock into a large pan and bring to a gentle simmer.

2 Melt 30g (1oz) of the butter in a large pan, add the onion, garlic and 2 bay leaf halves and sauté for 5–8 minutes until soft. Stir in the rice. Cook, stirring, for about 30 seconds.

3 Gradually add the stock, a ladleful at a time, to the rice, stirring and adding more stock as each batch is absorbed. The total cooking time will be about 20 minutes, at the end of which the rice should be *al dente*. Season well to taste. Set aside.

4 Meanwhile, cook the peas and mint together in a saucepan with some water, then remove and strain. Add the peas and mint to a blender and blitz to make a paste.

5 Keep 8 of the scallops to one side and cut the rest into medium-sized pieces. Return the risotto to a low heat and stir in the remaining butter. Add the pea and mint purée and the scallops, parsley and chives, cook for 4 minutes and season to taste. Discard the bay leaf halves.

6 Meanwhile, heat a griddle pan until smoking, sprinkle with salt and then pan fry the remaining 8 scallops for 1 minute each side.

7 Spoon the risotto into 4 large warmed bowls and place 2 seared scallops on each plate.

1 You will need a special oyster knife in order to open oysters without cutting your hand open at the same time!

2 Push the knife through the small gap between the hinge, and twist until the hinge breaks.

3 Open the shell gently, using the knife to cut through any remaining muscle.

4 Slide the knife under the oyster and free it from the shell, taking care to retain the oyster juices.

Oyster tempura

If I am going to cook oysters, this is the way I prefer: nice and fluffy – lovely! You could also serve this dish with a sweet chilli sauce – it makes a great snack before a dinner party.

SERVES: 4

Preparation time: 10 minutes plus 25 minutes resting time for batter
Cooking time: 4 minutes

300g (10½oz) rice flour
1 level teaspoon salt
1 egg, beaten
700ml bottle of sparkling water
24 rock oysters in ½ shell
vegetable oil for frying
2 limes, cut into wedges
100ml (3½fl oz) soy sauce
1 tablespoon chopped coriander

method

1 In a large bowl mix 225g (8oz) of the flour, the salt and egg and then add the water a little at a time until the batter is smooth. Leave to cool in the fridge for 25 minutes.

2 Take the oysters out of the shell and coat them in the remaining flour, then dip them in the batter, making sure they are completely covered.

3 Heat the oil to about 170°C (340°F) and fry the battered oysters for about 3–4 minutes until crispy. Serve with lime wedges, soy sauce and chopped coriander.

Oysters on ice with shallots, red wine vinegar and lemon

Raw oysters are one of those shellfish that you either love or hate. If you have never eaten a raw oyster before, make sure that you squeeze lemon juice on it and watch to make sure it contracts before you eat it.

SERVES: 4

Preparation time: 10 minutes plus
   2 hours chilling time

salt
4 turns freshly ground black pepper
150ml (5fl oz) red wine vinegar
3 tablespoons good red wine
10 shallots, finely chopped
crushed ice to serve
24 native oysters
2 lemons, halved

method

1 Make the shallot dressing by combining ½ teaspoon of salt, pepper, vinegar, wine and shallots in a bowl. Leave in the fridge for at least 2 hours.

2 Place some crushed ice on 4 serving plates and sprinkle with salt to prevent it melting too quickly. Make sure the oysters are freed from the shell, then place each on a half shell on top of the crushed ice. Serve with lemon halves and individual bowls of the shallot dressing.

Index

Page numbers preceded by the abbreviation (alt) denote the fish is listed as an alternative

Adriatic fish stew 144
American clam 122
American lobsters 121
Anchovy(ies) 72, (alt) 86, (alt) 92
    marinated 94

Baby smoked herring with beetroot and sour cream 100
Baked cod with black olive crust and lentils 21
Baked stuffed sardines 83
Baking in parchment 61
Barbecued red emperor with herb relish 116
Barbecued salmon with potato salad 80
Barbecued trout in newspaper 82
Barracuda 104, (alt) 115
    shiitake teriyaki 116
Barramundi 104
    with shellfish, braised 115
Black cod 12, (alt) 28
Black-shell mussels 122
Boneless herring dipped in egg and fried in garlic butter 92
Boning sardines, cleaning and 86
Bouillabaisse, gurnard 34
Braised barramundi with shellfish 115
Breading sole or other fish fillets 68
Bream 12, (alt) 13, (alt) 32, (alt) 105, (alt) 108
    stuffed with thyme and pan fried in lemon oil 18
    red (alt) 106
    sea (alt) 110
Brill 52
    Mediterranean-style 53
Brochettes, mixed seafood 88
Brown shrimp 121
Butterfish *see* Pomfret
Butterflying tiger prawns 124

Canadian lobsters 121
Carp 12
    poached in beer 31
Catfish 12
    in cornmeal 36
Clam(s) 122, (alt) 146
    hot pot, large American 148

in their own juice 148
with Oriental herbs and noodles, razor 147
see also Palourde(s)
Cleaning
    and boning sardines 186
    and filleting mackerel 74
    and filleting salmon 76
    and gutting round fish 14
    and scaling snapper 106
    see also Preparing
Coalfish *see* Coley
Cockles 122
Cod 12, (alt) 27, (alt) 31, (alt) 42, (alt) 69, (alt) 80, (alt) 115, (alt) 116
    with black olive crust and lentils, baked 21
    caldeirada, salt 40
    and chips, deep-fried 38
    fish cakes with parsley sauce, salt 42
    fish pie 37
    in teriyaki and orange 28
Codling (alt) 27, (alt) 31, (alt) 69
Coley 12, (alt) 27
    sour orange 31
Common crab 120, (alt) 143
Common mussels 122
Common shrimp 121
Crab(s) 120, (alt) 124, (alt) 133, (alt) 143
    claws pan fried with pesto 142
    Creole 141
    meat (alt) 42, (alt) 126
    preparing 140
Crayfish 120
    ravioli 130
    salad with mango and citrus dressing 133
Creole crab 141

Diver scallops St Jacques 150
Dolphin fish *see* Dorade
Dorade 104, (alt) 116
    poached in milk with herb sauce 112
Dorset crab 120
Dover sole (alt) 24, 52, (alt) 54
    fillets Dijon 56
    with peas and tomato sauce 54
Dublin Bay prawns *see* Langoustines

Eel 72
    endive and trevisano salad, smoked 98
European lobsters 121

Farmed salmon (alt) 85
    see also Salmon
Filleting
    flat fish 56
    John Dory 22
    mackerel, cleaning and 74
    round fish 20
    salmon, cleaning and 76
Fish cakes with parsley sauce, salt cod 42
Fish pie 35
Fish stew, Adriatic 144
Flat fish (alt) 56
    skinning and filleting 56
    see also names of fish
Flounder 52
    with grapes, sultanas and balsamic vinegar 62
Fried lemon sole with tomato sauce 68
Fried whitebait with paprika 92
Frying fish fillets 36

Gravadlax, making 95
    spring onion pancakes with 94
Grayling (alt) 13, (alt) 16
Grey mullet (alt) 14, (alt) 34, (alt) 110
Grilled squid with sweet chilli sauce and rocket 49
Grilled langoustines 129
Grilled red mullet with bay leaves 13
Gurnard 12
    bouillabaisse 34
Gutting round fish 14

Haddock 12, (alt) 61, (alt) 94, (alt) 98
    and avocado mousse, smoked 44
    fish pie 35
    tahini baked 27
Halibut 52, (alt) 115
    with lemon, red onion and coriander 66
    with saffron sauce and stewed leeks 64
Herring 72, (alt) 73, (alt) 83
    with beetroot and sour cream, baby smoked 100

dipped in egg and fried in garlic butter, boneless 92
rolled and filled 84

John Dory 12, (alt) 27, (alt) 110
    filleting 22
    with tapenade, mash and spinach 22

King prawns 121, (alt) 134, (alt) 136
    Portuguese style 125
King scallops 122

Langoustine(s) 121, (alt) 125
    bisque 128
    grilled 129
    preparing 128
Large American clam hot pot 148
Lemon sole 52, (alt) 54
    in parchment 61
    rolls stuffed with leeks, carrots and prawns 58
    with tomato sauce, fried 68
Lobster(s) 121, (alt) 124, (alt) 128
    burgers with chilli relish 138
    in Grand Marnier and kumquat sauce 138
    preparing 134
    thermidor 134
    with spaghetti 136

Mackerel (alt) 21, (alt) 44, 72
    Californian style 74
    cleaning and filleting 74
    with mustard and lemon butter 73
    pâté, spicy 98
    smoked (alt) 101
Mahi mahi *see* Dorade
Marinated anchovies 94
Marlin 104
    with black pepper and cream sauce 113
Mediterranean prawns 121
Mediterranean-style brill 53
Mixed fish, roast 86
Mixed seafood brochettes 88
Monkfish 12, (alt) 78, (alt) 115, (alt) 116
    tails (alt) 16
    wrapped in Chinese leaves, spiced 33
    wrapped in smoked pancetta 22

Mullet 12, (alt) 16, (alt) 18, (alt) 105, (alt) 116
see also Grey mullet, Red mullet
Mussels 122
diablo 145
with herb breadcrumbs, gratinated 146
preparing 144

Native oyster 122
Norway lobsters see Langoustines

Octopus (alt) 47
Oriental roast sea bass 14
Oriental squid 45
Oyster(s) 122
on ice with shallots, red wine vinegar and lemon 157
preparing 156
tempura 156

Pan frying whole fish 110
Pan-fried perch with béarnaise sauce 21
Pan-fried scallops 153
Palourdes 122, (alt) 147
Parrot fish (alt) 16, 104
with red curry paste 108
Perch 12
with béarnaise sauce, pan-fried 21
Pilchards see Sardines
Pink shrimp 121
Plaice 52, (alt) 53, (alt) 54, (alt) 58, (alt) 68
goujons in sparkling wine batter 69
Poaching 31
Pollock see Coley
Pomfret 104
with tamarind and chilli sauce 105
Potted brown shrimp 126
Prawn(s) 121, (alt) 129
butterflying tiger 124
curry, Thai 123
Dublin Bay see Langoustines
soufflé 124
Portuguese style, king 123
soufflé 124
see also King prawns, Mediterranean prawns
Preparing
crab 140
langoustine 128
lobster 134

mussels 144
oysters 156
scallops 150
squid 46
see also Cleaning

Queen scallops 122

Rainbow trout (alt) 80
Ravioli, making 136
Razor clam(s) 122
with Oriental herbs and noodles 147
Red bream (alt) 106
Red emperor 104
with herb relish, barbecued 116
Red mullet with bay leaves, grilled 13
Red snapper 12, (alt) 74, (alt) 106
sesame baked 16
Roast mixed fish 86
Rock oyster 122

Saithe see Coley
Salmon (alt) 42, (alt) 44, (alt) 64, 72, (alt) 74, (alt) 96, (alt) 112, (alt) 115
with bok choi and soy sauce 79
carpaccio with pine nuts and soy sauce 97
cleaning and filleting 76
farmed (alt) 85
parcel 77
with potato salad, barbecued 80
slicing 97
smoked (alt) 94
steaks, cutting 80
stuffed with crab and spinach with dill sauce 77
Salmon trout (alt) 77
Salt cod
caldeirada 40
fish cakes with parsley sauce 42
Sardines 72, (alt) 73, (alt) 92
baby (alt) 94
baked stuffed 83
cleaning and boning 86
with Sicilian spaghetti 90
smoked (alt) 100
Sashimi of sea bass 44
Scaling snapper, cleaning and 106
Scallop(s) (alt) 97, 122, (alt) 125, (alt) 129
ceviche with ginger, chilli, spring onions and soy 152

pan-fried 153
preparing 150
risotto with pea and mint 154
St Jacques, diver 150
Scottish lobsters 121
Sea bass 12, (alt) 18, (alt) 28, (alt) 33, (alt) 82, (alt) 108
Oriental roast 14
sashimi of 44
with Thai herbs, steamed 32
Sea bream (alt) 110
with mozzarella and pancetta 27
Sea trout and noodle salad 80
Seafood brochettes 88
Seafood risotto 130
Seared tuna with sticky rice, wasabi and soy sauce 96
Sesame baked red snapper 16
Shad 12
stuffed with sorrel and served with beurre blanc 18
Shark 104
steaks Moroccan style 115
Shrimp 121, (alt) 128, (alt) 133
with brandy pâté 126
potted brown 126
Skate 52
with black butter 54
Skinning
and filleting flat fish 56
salt cod 38
Slicing salmon 97
Smoked eel, endive and tevisano salad 98
Smoked haddock and avocado mousse 44
Smoked herring with beetroot and sour cream, baby 100
Smoked mackerel (alt) 101
Smoked salmon (alt) 94
Smoked sardines (alt) 100
Smoked trout (alt) 98
and potato salad 101
Snapper (alt) 13, (alt) 16, (alt) 115, (alt) 116
cleaning and scaling 106
see also Red snapper, Yellowtail snapper
Soft-shell crab 120
Sole (alt) 53
breading 68
see also Dover sole, Lemon sole
Sour orange coley 31

Spiced monkfish wrapped in Chinese leaves 33
Spicy baked yellowtail snapper with pine nuts 106
Spicy mackerel pâté 98
Spider crab 120
with linguine and courgettes 143
Sprats (alt) 92, (alt) 94
Spring onion pancakes with gravadlax 94
Squid 12
with gluten-free linguine and monkfish 49
large (alt) 47
Oriental 45
preparing 46
and spicy Italian sausage stew 48
with sweet chilli sauce and rocket, grilled 47
Steamed sea bass with Thai herbs 32
Stuffing a whole fish 19
Swordfish (alt) 33, (alt) 67, 72, (alt) 113, (alt) 115
paillard on Caesar salad 78

Tahini baked haddock 26
Thai prawn curry 113
Tiger prawns (alt) 45, 121
butterflying 124
Tilapia 104
with fruit sauce 110
Trout (alt) 31, 72, (alt) 79
with apples, cider and cream 85
and noodle salad, sea 80
and potato salad, smoked 101
rainbow trout (alt) 80
smoked (alt) 98
wrapped in newspaper 82
see also Salmon trout
Tuna (alt) 21, (alt) 33, (alt) 36, (alt) 44, 72, (alt) 74, (alt) 78, (alt) 113
with sticky rice, wasabi and soy sauce, seared 96
Turbot 52, (alt) 62, (alt) 66
with beetroot and potato rosti 62
hollandaise 67

Whitebait 72
with paprika, fried 92
Wrapping fish fillets in pancetta 24

Yellowtail snapper 104
with pine nuts, spicy baked 106

Acknowledgements

First and foremost, thank you to all of you who have bought this book. I hope you enjoy it as much as I enjoyed writing it. Nevertheless, if it wasn't for my publisher, Jacqui Small, getting together with my agent, Fiona Lindsey, this would never have happened, so thanks to you both.

A huge thanks to my wife, Nikki, for putting up with my weekends working in my office at home, working on holidays and even on the plane!

Thanks to my long-lasting PA, Luisa, for working wonders with all my scribbles and testing the recipes, so now she can apply for a home economist job!

And thanks to David Munns for being the most patient photographer I have ever met!

Big thanks to all at Billingsgate Fish Market and Borough Market for all their help.